Life Through the Eyes of a Red Headed, Wide-Eyed, Full Time Evangelist

Kay Osban

Copyright © 2013 Kay Osban
All rights reserved.
ISBN-10:148483464X
ISBN-13: 978-1484834640

Table of Contents

Dedication..iv

Foreword

    Robert F. Davis, Jr. and Maryann Davis........................... 1

    Jerri Sweatt..4

Acknowledgements.. 5

Chapter 1

    Frank and Jessie James... 9

Chapter 2

    Growing Up in a Valley...13

Chapter 3

    I Will Not Go! I Will Not!..21

Chapter 4

    Packing Up Is Hard To Do..30

Chapter 5

    Please, No More Chicken Noodle Soup..........................38

Chapter 6

    Family, Together Again!...44

Chapter 7

    A Mountain Top Experience..56

Chapter 8

    Let's Have A Revival!..63

Chapter 9

    Diary Of A Broken Ankle...90

Chapter 10

   It Could Only Happen To Me..97

Chapter 11

   Kids! I Love 'Em!..116

Chapter 12

   I Have Crazy Friends..125

Chapter 13

   My Family Doesn't Suffer From Insanity, We Rather Enjoy It!..154

Chapter 14

   Popular Messages...168

Chapter 15

   My Favorite Recipes..180

DEDICATION

MY ANGEL, IN WAL-MART PARKING LOT

It was a sunny day on a February afternoon in Jacksonville, Florida. My friend Lois and I had bought what we needed, got in the car and was backing out. Lois drew my attention to a tall, nice looking black man that was walking toward the front of my car while pointing at it.

I began to roll my window down, then hesitated as I remembered the email I had just read about not rolling down your window for strangers. But I felt a calm about this *stranger* and continued.

He said, "I like your licenses plate - He's still saving lives." My plate had a picture of Jesus that read, "He's still saving lives". I said, "Yes, He is." I was about to proceed backing out when his very presence seemed to say *wait*.

He continued, "You tell everyone you meet that *He* is still saving lives." I signify by nodding my head yes. He then said, "You have a very giving heart. This year the Lord is going to give you more, so *you* can give more."

I had just preached a message at Flatwoods, Virginia, "I give to get, to get to give." He then made a statement, in a matter of fact way, "You believe in angels." I said yes. But I was thinking, "I might be speaking to one right now!" He continued, "Angels are all around you, and you will win many souls to Him this year. You will touch many souls through your speaking engagements."

Now, at that moment I looked NOTHING like a speaker, as this was a Saturday and I was wearing a sweatshirt and blue jeans. I wondered how he knew I spoke, or that I was an Evangelist?

Now what I am about to tell you, nearly blew me away! The past several years I had been compiling a book. Hardly anyone knew about this, especially this man/angel in Wal-Mart parking lot!

He said, "You need to finish your book." Alright, now I have goose bumps all up and down me! I told him that I had been dragging my feet. He said, "Yes, but you need to finish it. The book will be a great success, and it too will touch many lives."

My foot is on the brake, *CAUSE I AIN'T GOING NOWHERE!* I wondered if I was dreaming! In my travels across this beautiful America, I have taken many gorgeous pictures. I had *thought* about putting one of my *scenery* pictures on the front of the book. In fact, that was going through my mind, when all of a sudden he said, (as though he was reading my very thoughts!) "No, no. Not that picture. *Your* picture is to be on the front cover." I said, "O K" (While thinking, "I want the book to sell!") His instructions were very detailed.

I felt like I was talking face to face with God Himself! I asked a favor of him. "Will you pray for me? I am going to South Carolina tomorrow to sing and speak at a friend's funeral." He said, in a stern voice, "You will do well!" I replied, "But I have a bad sinus infection." At this point I felt like Moses - full of excuses.

With that said, immediately he stretched his hand out toward me (he had never made an attempt to touch me) and he began praying, "I bind up this sinus infection, and I loose her from it! Satan, you have no power over her. No weapon that is formed against her shall prosper; and every tongue that shall rise against her in judgment shall be condemned."

He prayed a long prayer. I can't remember every thing he said, but I remember not wanting the prayer to come to an end. He looked into the car and saw my friend, Lois. He began speaking to her, "You also have a giving heart. I see a caring, nursing, spirit about you."

I told him that in a few months, Lois was going to have major surgery on her back. I asked, "Will you pray for her also?" As long as I live, I will *NEVER* forget the look of compassion that flowed from him. I mean it! His eyes had compassion that seemed to flow out of him like a stream of peaceful waters. I have never seen anything like it before!

He stretched his hand toward Lois and began to pray a prayer of healing for her. He prayed for the doctors and nurses, for God to guide their hands.

It was a beautiful prayer. When he finished, he looked straight at her and spoke these words, "Everything is going to go well. Sometimes God chooses to heal through doctors, but it will be well."

He stepped back as though to say, "I'm finished now". We thanked him for his prayers, kindness, and the words of encouragement. He nodded, and walked away.

I was still in a state of shock as I backed out of my parking space. I looked over at Lois and said, "WOW! I feel like we just had a visit from God!"

I have often wished that I would have watched him as he walked away. Because it would not have surprised me one little bit, to have watched him disappear into thin air! Since that day, I simply refer to him as "My Angel!"

Ask yourself this question, how could he have known I was writing a book? AND! How did he know what picture I was thinking about putting on the cover of the book? Personally, I will always believe he was an Angel sent by God!

By the way, I went on to the funeral. It was being held in a church. While the family was in the basement of the church eating, I went upstairs to practice my song. I could not hit that one high note to save my life! I thought, "Oh well, I am here and I am going to just do the best I can."

When it came time for me to sing, it was as though Angels took hold of my vocal cords and sang through them! I never struggled a bit and I hit that high note with so much ease. My sinus was healed completely! I immediately thought of the words *my Angel* had spoken to me in a Wal-Mart parking lot, "It will be well!" And it was!

After the funeral, my friend Jerri Sweatt asked, "Will you go find that Angel and ask him to come pray for my voice so I can sing like that?" On a personal note, Jerri always sings like that! But for me that day, it was God!

With that said, I would like to dedicate this book to the Angel in the Wal-Mart parking lot. For without him speaking to me on that day, I may have never finished my book.

FOREWORD

It is indeed a delight to write a foreword to this book. Every one of us encounters many different situations in life. Kay Osban is a person that has a very unique ability. She is able to take the things she encounters and put it in a positive light and in most cases give it a humorous twist.

I have known her from the beginning of her ministry and she is deeply committed to her faith. She lives what she preaches. And she has had a tremendous effect on those she ministers too.

She is a very gifted minister as well as talented musician and singer. There is no doubt in my mind that she could have pursued opportunities in the secular sense, but she chose to dedicate her life, energies and talent to God and his service.

Her life, as with any of us has not all been easy. But with all her many adventures, she always continued on with a smile while bringing laughter and joy to the lives of those to which she ministered.

There have been times in her life when I couldn't see how she could make it, but she did. She never let anything stop her from serving the Savior she loves so much. When difficulty came, she would just emerge herself in prayer and come forth with renewed strength to continue on in her journey home. Her heart was given to helping others and making it easier for them to make it. Not many have ever seen her tears. But, then, maybe that was as it should be, reserved for God and Him alone.

Kay loved her family with a faithfulness not often seen in our world. And as it has turned out, the scripture in Matthew 19:29 has been fulfilled in her life. It says, "And every one that hath forsaken houses, or brethren, or sisters, or father, or mother, or wife, or children, or lands, for my name's sake, shall receive an hundredfold, and shall inherit everlasting life."

I can say without reservation that Kay Osban can travel all over the United States and *never* have to find a motel, because she has people everywhere that love her like family and would without reservation open their home to her anytime she needed a place to stay.

Let me conclude with a smile as I think of you reading this book. Life's not easy, but this book will lighten your load.

Lifetime Friends in Christ,

-Bishop, Dr., Robert F. Davis Jr.
and
Maryann Davis

FOREWORD

What a privilege it has been to have a friend like Kay for several decades. She has always been a Christ-centered, fun loving lady that has proven you can have a wonderful time living for the King of Kings.

Kay was called into the ministry by God to be an evangelistic blessing and soul gatherer for Him. Her life has been wholly dedicated to God when it was not popular to do so. Her sense of humor has been medicinal to many a soul. Her music and singing has blessed and uplifted so many.

I can remember visiting Kay and her family, her dad and mom, Willie and Jessie James (yes, her mom was kin to the infamous Jesse James) Osban in Hoopa with her brother Rick and sister Margie. What a blessing and a privilege it was to be invited to their home. Her dad was a tall lumberjack, and they lived up north on an Indian Reservation in California and quite far from the other churches, but no worries, they had their own in-house entertainment complete with piano, guitars, singing and a delicacy of smoked salmon. Great memories. Great fun. Great family who loved God. Quite a legacy.

Paul tells us in 1Timothy 6:6 "But Godliness with contentment is great gain". He also reminded Timothy, a young minister, that having food and raiment to be therewith content. This is my friend, Kay. No grandeur, just a servant of the most High, fulfilling her calling. If she is in youth camp full of teenagers, teaching minister's wives, speaking at conventions, singing on TBN and even babysitting little ones, she is content. Evangelizing, Pastoring, Speaking, Singing, Playing Music, Christian Comedian, she is content. This is great gain.

She experienced a calling from God on her life, and at the age of 18 was licensed in The Church of God of Prophecy. She studied, prepared herself and hasn't stopped going forward since. Her ministry has taken her throughout twenty seven or so states where she has made many friends and experienced God's saving power in rescuing sinners.

This friend of mine has been an inspiration to those that have attended her meetings. The sense of humor God gave her is a testimony to her healthy lifestyle through the years..."a merry heart doeth good like a medicine..." Proverbs 17:22. Her life hasn't been without tragedy, but she has learned to be content and happy working for the Master.

Her love of fishing and preparing them hasn't stopped since she has been doing God's work. As a fisher of fish, she catches them alive and they become dead. As a fisher of men, she catches them dead and they become alive.

Keep on being an inspiration Kay, being content, ministering and fishing. Our Lord was a fisher of men also! I'm sure her book will be a blessing to you.

Jerri Sweatt, Friend
Modesto, California

ACKNOWLEDGEMENTS

First of all, I thank my Savior Jesus Christ for all He has done for me! I am not ashamed to say that He is the love of my life! I live for Him alone.

Thanks to my parents, I was raised in a Christian home. Mom and dad taught me right from wrong. They taught me to love God and to treat others as I would like to be treated. When I was growing up, we may not have had all the frills that the world had to offer, but we had love! Daddy was a hard working man. Mama was a hard working housewife.

Jeremy Dierks helped make this project possible. He spent countless hours editing, proof reading, and rereading this book. I can never thank him enough for his labor of love!

Debbie Hostetler was a great help with her artistic illustrations. She does amazing drawings! Thank you Debbie!

Thanks to Robert F. Davis Jr. for the Photography Art used in the cover design.

To all my friends. Those who have been cheering me on to complete this book, thank you! Trudie Lee kept pushing me, and for that, I am thankful! Sometimes we just need a little push, a little encouragement and a whole lot of love!

I have what I like to call *"encouragers"* in my life. I have had many over the past thirty-five-years. Those who encouraged me to *hang in there* when the going got tough. Encouraged me to listen to God, preach what *He* wanted, and not to be pleasers of any other.

It would be impossible to name everyone in this book, or to tell everything everyone has done for me. If I fail to adequately say what you mean to me, I ask that you forgive me. But you know who you are, and that is most importance. Please know that I love you all!

INTRODUCTION

Edwin Hubbell Chapin was a preacher from the early 1800's. He is famous for many quotes. I happen to like this one:

"Every action in our lives touches on some chord that will vibrate in eternity".

As I have endeavoured to fulfill God's will for *my* life, I can only pray that my actions have touched lives that will vibrate throughout eternity. I sure have enjoyed traveling across the United States, just me, the Lord and my guitar!

I do not know how many messages I have preached over the past forty years, thirty-five of those years being full-time. The countless miles I have travelled, mostly by car. I've lost track of how many vehicles I have worn out for the gospel. I can relate to the words of the song that Vestal Goodman use to sing, "I Don't Regret a Mile I've Traveled For the Lord." And I don't.

I have a motto that I live by, it's a simple motto:

"If my life doesn't make a difference, then what difference does it make?"

Our lives must count for something. We truly were born to serve the Lord. Most of the time, serving the Lord involves serving one another. I strive to be the life that is *"Sold out, the whole route"* in my service to God.

Jude the 23rd verse really speaks to my spirit. *"And others save with fear, pulling them out of the fire;…"*

You see, I do not want anyone going to hell. I have had many straight-forward talks with a lot of folks while down here on this earth. Not wanting to hurt their feelings, but at the same time, I do not want to baby them into hell.

I have a reputation of *"being vocal"*. In that, I'm not talking about being rude or harsh. I believe the Lord's return is so soon, that I want everyone I come into contact with to be ready.

Recently, I was preaching at Palm Harbor, Florida, where Brother Scott Creasy is the Pastor. As I was ministering, I felt God's Spirit tell me, "My coming is so close, you can feel my breath on the back of your neck". I think I was supposed to tell the congregation what He spoke to me, but it stunned me so, that I just stood there speechless!

A few months later, I was ministering at North Tazewell, Virginia, where Brother McLemore is the Pastor. We were up at the front praying for different ones.

I was standing about six feet back from those who were praying. All of a sudden, I felt a blast of cool air hit the back of my neck and circle around to the front of my neck.

I immediately looked behind me to see who it might be, but no one was near me. I looked up to see where the vents for the air flow were, but they were in the floor, and not anywhere around me.

In a moment's time, the Spirit of God reiterated to me again, "My coming is so close, you can feel my breath on the back of your neck". I cannot explain the anticipation that goes through me just thinking about it. Anticipating going to be with the Lord, and yet feeling apprehensive, or dread for all those who are not yet ready for His return. I guess you could call it *"bitter sweet"*.

I really believe that if we knew how close the coming of Christ is, we would certainly do more, pray more and talk to those who are lost more. What a privilege it is to be able to lead someone to Jesus Christ! It is great joy to hear them testify of what God has done for them. They tell of how *differently* they feel. It's as though they can't really explain it. There is no greater feeling than this!

I was thinking the other day about how life consists of *"finishes"*. In the mornings, we finish our prayers; we finish our breakfast and finish getting ready for the day.

Then we finish our work, or school. We come home and finish the evening dinner and finish getting ready for bed. Then we start it all over again the next day.

The apostle Paul talks about the greatest finish that there is, our *life*. Listen to what he says in 2 Timothy 4:8-9.

"I have fought a good fight, I have *finished* my course, I have kept the faith.

Henceforth there is laid up for me a crown of righteousness, which the Lord, the righteous judge, shall give me at that day: and not to me only, but unto all them also that love his appearing."

My prayer is for all of us to finish well! A good fight is a fight where you win. Live your life as it would be pleasing to God.

I have asked God to spend me, and use me in any way that He wants to. I want my Bible to be worn out and my life completely *worn out* for Him! For I believe that this is the way it truly should be.   - Kay Osban

Kay on TBN

CHAPTER 1
FRANK AND JESSIE JAMES

I have decided to start in the beginning. My mother was born to Frank and Elsie James in Greenfield, Arkansas. They had thirteen children of which mom was the fourth born. The first born was a girl, then a boy, then another girl, and then mom.

I've never figured out why they never named their first boy, Jessie. But the name seemed to suit mom just fine. She was a great shot with a gun for sure!

Since this was the early 1900's, they had no car and walking was their only transportation. When folks would see grandpa and mom walking into town, they'd laugh and say, "Here comes Frank and Jessie James!"

My grandpa, Frank James, was born in 1895. The outlaw Frank James was born 1843 and died in1915. So my mom and her family lived during the era that the tales of the notorious outlaws "The James Gang" were flying around. The first movie my mom ever saw was "Frank and Jesse James". She said it cost a whole nickel to get in!

I've never researched my family tree for fear that I would find too many of them *hanging* in them! I have heard that we are related to "The James Gang". I know this is a great surprise to many of you! Even if we are not related to the James Gang, I can truthfully say, "I am the granddaughter and daughter of Frank and Jessie James!"

There were times when I would hear mom and her sisters telling about their childhood, the things they did, the trouble they got into, and I would think, "I wish I had lived back then".

But as they continued about how hot the sun was as they were picking cotton on grandma and grandpa's eighty acre farm, working from can to cain't; I quickly decided that

I would choose *now* instead of *then*. Can you imagine days without cell phones? It actually sounds kind of nice.

I remember asking mom and her siblings, "Tell me about the good ole days". They'd all laugh and say, "They weren't good ole days. It was hard working days!" Then they'd start telling about the pranks they had played on each other.

Like the time they were all working out in the field picking cotton (I came from a cotton picking family!) and mom thought it would be funny to pretend she fainted.

She was all the way down at the end of her row and she just fell over. Her brother Benny and sister Evalyn dropped their sacks and ran like crazy all the way down to the end where mom had supposedly fainted. As they grabbed a hold of her, she began to laugh uncontrollably. They nearly beat the snot out of her!

Then there was the time she had a hold of one end of a crosscut saw and her sister had the other end. As she watched her sister push the saw towards her, the handle would be raised up. But when mom pushed it back to her, her sisters handle would be down and her nose would be a couple inches from it. Mom thought how funny it would be to jerk her handle down, thus knocking her sister's handle up and hitting her in the nose. So mom did it, but it hit harder than mom had intended, and gave her sister a bloody nose! Mom got into trouble over that one.

Her brother Bennie decided he was going to catch a skunk. When he did, he was determined to remove the stinker from the skunk. He stuck the skunks head down into a boot and began the operation. Before he could get the stink sack removed, he got sprayed. But he persevered until the sack was out of the skunk. Mom said Bennie stunk so bad that they had to bury his clothes!

Since the skunk could no longer spray, they made a pet out of it. They said when the skunk would want to be a little stinker (sorry, I couldn't help the pun) and spray them, he would run and put his front feet down and his tail up, but nothing would come out.

Here is a little funny to go with that story:

Mama skunk worried because she couldn't keep track of her two baby skunks whose names were *In* and *Out*.

One day she called Out in to her and told him to go out and bring In back. So Out went out and soon brought In in. Mama skunk asked, "How could you find him so quickly in this great forest?" Out said, "It was simple, In-stinct."

Life must have been very hard growing up on that eighty-acre farm. Grandpa and Grandma's first child, Floragean, died early on at the age of eleven months.

Then the last child born, Everett Lee, died at the age of two. Before Grandma died, she had buried five of her children. They say that parents should never have to bury one of their children.

It was after Everett Lee's death that salvation came to Frank James. Mom's cousin, L.T. Morris was a minister in The Church of God of Prophecy. He came and talked to Grandpa about accepting Jesus Christ as his Lord and Savior.

Up to that time, Grandpa had been a drinking man. But he put it all away for this new life in Christ! He took off the old man, and put on the new!

Grandpa lived another two years before dying with a heart attack. I was only two-years old. I never got to know my Grandpa.

When I was a young adult, Grandma was telling me about Grandpa. She said, "Kay, when you were born Frank took you in his arms and said, "Elsie, have you ever seen a more beautiful baby!" I love that man! I hope all the other grandkids don't get jealous. Lol

When Grandpa died, Grandma still had six kids left at home to raise, Betty, Patsy, Paul, Dickie, Diane and Chris. Bennie, Evalyn, Jessie, Euphemia, and Augustine were already married. I know what you are thinking… where did they come up with some of these names? One aunt told me the midwives named some of them. I won't even begin to tell you their middle names!

Out of that James family would come two licensed ministers, Bennie James and Jessie Osban. Uncle Bennie would go on to pastor several churches in Arkansas, Arizona and Missouri. Mom would pastor Hoopa, California. Both were great ministers.

CHAPTER 2
GROWING UP IN A VALLEY
WHILE LIVING ON A MOUNTAIN TOP!

My dad, Willie Dean Osban was born in 1931, at Bradford, Arkansas. Mom, Jessie James Osban was born in 1932 at Greenfield, Arkansas. Dad went in the Army, serving in Korea in 1951 until January of 1952. He made Corporal. He got out of the Army later that year.

Dad and Mom were married in 1952. They lived in Gibson Switch, Arkansas while dad worked on a farm. My brother, Rick was born in Harrisburg, Arkansas in 1953.

From 1954-1955 they lived in Parma, Missouri where dad worked on a farm. They made a visit back to Greenfield, Arkansas while mom was in her ninth month of pregnancy with me. During that visit I was born in Harrisburg, Arkansas on February 6, 1955.

In 1956 we moved to Poplar Bluff, Missouri. Dad found work loading crossties. In 1957 we moved back to Greenfield, Arkansas, and once again dad worked on a farm.

1958 our family moved to Gramby, Colorado, and lived with dad's father, Bob Osban. He was a really nice Grandpa. He died when I was only nine.

Dad began cutting timber. Later that year, dad, mom, Rick and I packed up and moved to Fresno, California. This is where dad really began his career in the timber industry. Our family lived in logging camps such as, Dunlap and Dinkey Creek, California. People, you can't make these names up! Google it!

I was only three or four, but I remember that logging camp well. We lived in a cabin with an outhouse out back. One day I was in the outhouse and a chipmunk jumped on my head and was running around in my hair! I was screaming for my mama! Lets just say it didn't take me long to do my business.

There was a dirt road in front of our cabin. Across that road was a little grocery store. Wal-Mart had not even been thought of in 1959! Inside this store was a sign posted, "Please hang your firearms on the wall pegs".

Mom was the best mom ever! She would keep Rick and I occupied by playing games with us. Hand-held games had not been invented yet. I wish they had never been invented so kids could know what it is like to actually *"play"* a game, outside! When I was a kid growing up, a game boy was the boy next door who played games with you. That was a real game boy!

Ok, off my soapbox and back to the story. Someone had a horse named Cookie and mom would take turns letting us ride on it. We always took a nap in the afternoon.

One day mom said, "After we take our nap, we will go to the store and get an ice cream!" So all three of us laid on the bed for our nap. Well, I was so excited about that ice cream that I couldn't go to sleep!

I waited until mom and Rick fell asleep and I slipped off the bed. I walked across to the grocery store and got three ice creams. I laid them up on the counter and the lady rang them up. She said, "That will be fifteen cents."

I put my poor pitiful lying head down and said, "We ain't got no money because we are dirt poor." She just smiled and put them in a paper sack and handed them to me. She knew my mom would pay for them later.

I was ecstatic with joy! I ran across the road and into the cabin only to be met by mom. She was frantically looking for me. "Where have you been Paula Kay!" She always called me by my first name when she was mad at me. I was beaming from ear to ear as I pulled the three ice creams from the bag and exclaimed, "I was at the store. I got ice creams, one for Rick and you and me!"

Why didn't she have her happy face on? She looked perturbed as she questioned me. "And just where did you get the money to pay for them?" I said, "That's the best part, they were free!" I thought the happy face would appear... it did not.

She said, "I know they don't just give away ice creams. How did you get them?" I replied, "I told her we were poor, dirt poor!" I don't know why, but I thought this would produce a happy face, but it didn't. She put the ice creams back in the bag (by now, Rick is confused... he had an ice cream, and now he doesn't) and grabbed me by the hand and *jerked* me across the road to the store. My feet barely touched the ground all the way over there!

The lady smiled as mom placed the ice cream on the counter. It was at that point I realized it was all an *adult* trick. *Give the little girl what she wants, then let her mother take care of her!* I get it. After mom made me apologize to her, and making sure I told her we were *not* dirt poor, we once again took the ice cream across the road to the cabin. By now, even the ice cream was getting dizzy!

Then mom proceeds to tell me that she and Rick were going to eat their ice cream while I went to take my nap. I didn't really think it was fair. But who was I but a four-year-old little girl, up against a twenty-three-year-old mom. And I might add, a mom *without* a happy face!

It was at this same place, Dinkey Creek, California, that Rick and I got our first taste of a bar of soap. Mom walked outside just in time to hear us say *heck*. She grabbed us up and put the end of the soap in our mouth and told us to bite down. Boy howdy! Did you ever try to get bar soap out from between your teeth? The more you swish your tongue against your teeth, the more the bubbles foam. We looked like the mouth of that dog from "Old Yeller" frothing with foam! We were not allowed to use slang words.

Excuse me while I climb aboard the soapbox for a minute. Today I hear children using all kinds of slang and inappropriate language. We need more June Cleaver's (mother of The Beaver) and Sheriff Andy Taylor's in the home today. Instead we have Honey Boo Boo's! We didn't talk back to our parents either. TV has taught children what to say, and when to say it and how to say it. The 5th Commandment is, "Honor your father and your mother".

Excuse me while I climb down.

Ok, then we returned back to Fresno. It was here that mom and dad met their lifelong friends, Charlie and Wilma Gentle. They had two sons, Sammy and Eddie who were mine and Rick's age. The four of us had a lot of fun together.

One day Charlie looked at mom and said, "Jessie, you're pregnant." Mom was cooking mushrooms and lifted her spatula up and shook it at Charlie and said, "I am not!" Charlie said, "Well, if you are, and it's a girl, can I have her?" Mom replied, "Charlie, I'm not. But yes, if I am, and it's a girl, you can have her!"

So, seven months later, on September 21st, 1960, Margie was born. She was a precious bundle of joy for our parents. God knew mom needed a rest after putting up with Rick and me for five and six years! I remember telling my teacher, "When I get home, my baby sister will be there!" And she was. Although Charlie still claims Margie to this day, she never went to live with them.

Dad had a great opportunity for a job in northern California. By this time he was a bona fide timber faller. In August of 1962 the family moved to northern California to live on an Indian Reservation, Hoopa. That would be dad and mom's last move for many years.

I loved Hoopa! I loved the huge mountains that surrounded it and the Trinity River that flowed right through the middle of the valley. I would call this home for the next sixteen years. And most of all, I loved the people. A seven-year-old looks through the eyes of love and expects the best in everyone. I had as many Indian friends as I did White friends. I entered the 2nd grade there. I would go on to graduate from Hoopa High - home of the Mighty Warriors!

I had some really great teachers. Miss Gill was probably my favorite because she taught Gym. Everyone loved Ms. Gill. She also taught Drivers Ed. I know I scared the life out of her a few times just by seeing how fast I could take a sharp curve. But she always had her "chicken brake" on the passenger's side, just in case!

Hoopa Valley, California!

It was so much fun as a child growing up on the Reservation. There were two grocery stores, three gas stations, a post office and not one traffic light! It was like growing up in Mayberry. During the summer all the neighborhood kids would play outside until ten o'clock. Because there were no cell phones, if we were later than that, a mother would stand out on the porch and yell her child's name. That name would echo across the neighborhood.

We had a patch of woods behind our house that made for some really good hiding places when playing hide and go seek. Remember that game? How about Mumbley-Peg, or Red Rover, Red Rover or Annie, Annie over? That's when one person would stand in the front yard and the other in the backyard and have a ball the size of a soccer ball. The one with the ball would yell, "Annie, Annie over!" and throw the ball over the roof of the house. The person on the other side had to guess if the ball would come from the middle, the right or the left. They had to catch it before it hit the ground. Now, in your mind, you have to picture much smaller houses than those of today.

We'd play whiplash and get in a line and hold hands and the leader would run with everyone running behind him, still holding hands. He would run in a zigzag pattern. Well, the one at the end of the line would nearly have their feet off the ground! God sure did protect us from many broken bones.

Oh how I loved going to the football and basketball games there. Rick was an outstanding basketball player. He stood nearly 6'4" and was the forward-center for the Warriors. They even went All-State and won!

Dad wasn't one to go to the games. But mom was. We talked dad into going to one of Rick's games. It was the playoffs. The score was tight, the clock was running down and Rick put the ball in the air! It seemed like an eternity as it slowly headed towards the basket. There it was, nothing but net! Rick had hit a three pointer!

The gym became electrified as mom stood up and yelled to the top of her lungs, "THAT'S MY SON! YES HE IS!" Dad grabbed a hold of her shirttail and said, "Jessie, sit down!" She did, but in her heart she was standing up.

Sometimes our church would run the concession stand at the basketball games. The ladies made the most wonderful, mouth-watering yeast donuts that you have ever eaten. Glaze, coconut, banana nut and maple bars. They'd make your tongue slap your brains out! Goodness! I'd give a ten dollar bill for one right now! They would have easily put Krispy Kreme donuts out of business. And you know how much I love Krispy Kreme donuts!

Mom would be the chauffeur for many of the away games. She looked short sitting behind the wheel of that big ole Suburban. The team loved it when "Mrs. Osban" drove. Why? Because mom was the life of the party! I was allowed to go with them as well.

On one particular trip, mom slowed down and said, "There is a CHP". One of the players, Bob, asked her what is a CHP? Mom told him it stood for California Highway Patrol. Later on she slowed down again and said, "There's a C.O.P.". Bob said, "What's that Mrs. Osban?" Mom began to laugh and said, "Bob, C.O.P. is cop!" The bus burst out in laughter. Great memories.

After junior year was over, I immediately went to work at "Jordan's Shopping Center". I worked all summer long. Then during my senior year, I had enough credits that I only had to go to school until noon, and then I left and went to work at the store.

These six years of working there were some of the best memories in Hoopa. It gave me a chance to get acquainted with many of the adults in the Valley. One elderly gentleman (hey, when you're 18, anyone over 30 is elderly!) would put a smile on my face when he entered the door. That would be Mr. Jimmy Jackson! He was three-fourth Indian. He even taught me how to say a few words in his native tongue. He was the sweetest and most kind man. I was so sad a few years ago when Mr. Jackson passed away at the age of 93! Jimmy, I will never forget you.

His daughter, Mush also worked there. I became good friends with her family. In fact, we went back to Hoopa this past summer and Margie and I got to see all of them. Dooley (Laura) sent smoked salmon home with us. Now that's some good eating!!!

I had three bosses, Mr. Jordan and Boyd and Joyce Jury. They were the best bosses! They were very fair to their employees. If you worked at Jordan's, they made you feel like part of the family. We had a lot of laughs! You could always hear Boyd whistling throughout the store. He had a contagious laugh and a smile to match!

Little did I know that this season of working at Jordan's would soon be over and I would move to a land thousands of miles away.

CHAPTER 3
I WILL NOT GO! I WILL NOT!

"The Spirit of the Lord God is upon me; because the Lord hath anointed me to preach good tidings unto the meek; he hath sent me to bind up the brokenhearted, to proclaim liberty to the captives, and the opening of the prison to them that are bound;" Isa 61:1

At an early age, I began to feel the call of God on my life. I began doing some weekend revivals. My bosses at Jordan's were very accommodating of my schedule. Although I enjoyed these revivals, enjoyed seeing souls saved and saints uplifted by the Lord, I felt *secure* in my secular job.

I was licensed by The Church of God of Prophecy at the tender age of eighteen. I had given my heart to the Lord when I was only three-years-old. The Lord knew He had to get me early on! I joined the church when I was eight.

In the summer of 1978 God began to stir my heart towards Evangelism. I knew this stirring as I had felt it many times in my life when God was *up to something*. I kept feeling troubled in my spirit. The State Overseer from Oregon had called and offered me the position of State Evangelist. After much prayer, I knew this was not what God wanted. To tell the truth, I was relieved! Yes sir, living here in the valley with my family and friends suited me just fine!

I still remember looking out my bedroom window into the millions of stars, crying out to God for His will in my life. I so desperately wanted to do what He wanted me to do. I was only eighteen, but I loved the Lord with all of my heart.

I was sitting beside my mom at our annual State Convention in 1974. I was nineteen and had just graduated from Hoopa High the year before.

The State Overseer was making the yearly appointments of the pastors. I was writing down which pastor was going where. I had heard that we were going to get a new pastor for Hoopa and I was excited!

I diligently followed along in my program. The churches were alphabetized. He was getting closer to the "H's"! Who could it be? Oh God, please give us a pastor after Your own heart! We had all prayed so much for that.

There it was, he said "Hoopa... Kay Osban". I turned to my mom and said, "That scared me to death, I thought he said my name! Whose name did he really call?" Mom said, "He called your name, now get to the platform". To the platform? That's where all the pastors were to stand.

I promise you, I was so taken off guard! I never dreamed in a million years of being a pastor! My legs were weak as I walked to the platform. You can't even imagine what was going through my mind as I stood there with all the *real* pastors! Thoughts like, "Will I have to give up chewing gum?" No, not really. I can't remember what went through my mind. What would be going through yours?

I continued to work at the store while I pastored. I felt like more of a *pester* than a pastor! But it was a good year and the church did grow. But I felt like a fish out of water. As the next convention drew close, the Overseer wrote me and told me what a great job I had done and he was sure I'd want to stay on as pastor.

I wrote him back and told him that I was not a pastor, I was an evangelist. I ask him please *do not* call my name out as pastor again. I felt like I had served my time. To my relief, he listened. So, I was relieved as pastor and life went back to normal, whatever that is! I agree with whoever said that normal was just a setting on the dryer!

Hum, it seems I have digressed, gotten a little off track of the story I was telling you. So, back to the summer of 1978. Like I said, the Lord was stirring in me. I began to be burdened for Arkansas. Arkansas? Sure, I was born there. We went back to grannies almost every Christmas as a child, but Arkansas? I didn't know any pastor in that state except the one at Harrisburg. Arkansas? Thanks, but no thanks Lord.

I had already planned my vacation to go to Arkansas and visit with my relatives. I didn't even know who the State Overseer was. But God did. Once I arrived in Arkansas, God continued His pulling at me. Just to get Him off my back, I told God I would go by Little Rock and visit with the Overseer. I made the appointment and went.

Bishop H. M. Biggers was a giant of a man! He and his wife were the sweetest folks. She began cooking as soon as my feet were inside the state parsonage. And boy howdy she could cook!

I told Brother Biggers that I had *"thought"* about maybe one day returning to Arkansas to minister. He jumped right in with, "Well, I need a State Evangelist and I sure could use you!" I began making excuses (I sort of sounded like Moses) of how, outside of my relatives, I really didn't know anyone in Arkansas.

He pressed on. "I'll set you up with the first five revivals. That will get you started. I'll even guarantee you $50.00 a month!" I thought, "Wow, a whole $50.00 a month!"

This was 1978. The minimum wage was $2.65 an hour. I was making a little over $3.00 an hour. I did my math and figured I could make $50.00 in two days at Jordan's!

He continued to tell me there was a trailer house in Searcy that I could rent. Well, I had heard that tornados were God's way of saying don't live in a trailer house! But, since I wasn't really interested in moving to Arkansas anyway, I just listened.

Before I left, Brother Biggers said, "Now, the General Assembly is this September. They will be making appointments for the Overseers. I do not expect to be coming back to Arkansas, I expect to retire." Well, this put a whole new light on the subject. If he wasn't coming back, who on earth was? And would they be as nice as the Biggers were? Nope, this move definitely wasn't for me!

On my drive back to grannies, the Lord and I had a nice, and not so nice, long talk. I told God that I was happy right where I was living. I was renting from my parents, the rent was cheap and it wasn't a trailer house! AND, Hoopa had never had a tornado. Nope, I was a happy camper living right there in Hoopa.

I told God that I didn't want to leave my mom, dad, brother, sister and my little dog *Skeeter*. I didn't know these people in Arkansas. Why, He was asking me to go to a land that I knew not of. My name was Kay, not Moses!

We had quite a discussion. I reminded Him that Brother Biggers was not staying and he had only offered me five revivals to start with. Nope, not having it!

I told God I needed at least *twelve* revivals to get started. "You give me twelve, then we'll talk". I didn't tell anyone about this, afraid *they'd* make it happen.

My vacation had come to an end. The revivals still stood at five and I was happy. Maybe the Lord wasn't going to make me move after all. Not that I had anything against Arkansas, I just didn't want to leave my family in California.

My aunt Diane and I were going to Jonesboro to eat lunch and then I was heading back to California. The car was already packed.

As we were eating, my aunt said, "Kay, there is Brother Lawrence. He is the District Overseer here." He saw Diane and came over to the table and introductions were made. My aunt said, "Kay is an Evangelist. We'd like her to move to Arkansas to evangelize." I thought she could have kept that gem to herself!

Brother Lawrence said, "Well, come on! I've got twelve churches in my district, and I could set you up with that many revivals." *Twelve*? Did he just say *twelve*?

I felt God in my spirit laughing. I found it hard to finish my steak. I had made God a promise, and I believed in keeping my promises. That was something my dad had instilled in me.

Well, let's just say it was a long 2,300 miles back to Hoopa. All kinds of thoughts were rolling around inside of me. What if I can't make it? I don't want to lose my car. I have perfect credit and I don't want it ruined.

I began to bargain with God. Now, I do not advise this, it doesn't work. I told God that if it *really was* His will for me to leave Hoopa, then let Brother Biggers stay one more year as the Overseer of Arkansas. I promised Him I would do more work in the little local church in Hoopa, I'd give more and even tithe more than 10%! What a deal I was offering Him!

When I returned home to Hoopa, I only told my mom about what I felt like the Lord was speaking to me. Mom was so happy and told me she would help me pray about it. She made it clear that she would miss me, but she wanted me to be in God's will. She didn't make me feel like, "Here's your hat, what's your hurry?"

Mom was my balcony friend, always cheering me on. She was always in my corner, always had my back. But she was like that with all of us kids. She never made a difference. She wanted the very best for us, wanted us to be what God had intended us to be.

Allow me to reminisce about my mom for a moment. She was so much fun! She had a great outlook on life, a "you can do it" attitude. Mom was an encourager, not only to us, but to her friends.

She led her friend, Molly Cotton to Jesus. Molly was real bashful. Over the years, I watched as mom brought her out of that. Taught her to stand up for herself.

Molly was a great friend to mom and to the rest of our family as well.

One way I can relate to how it must be for those who have gone on to Heaven, is in this story. A few years after I had moved to Arkansas, I flew back to Arcata, California, for vacation. Mom and Margie came to the airport to pick me up.

At San Francisco I managed to get an earlier flight out to Arcata. Since there were no cell phones, I couldn't reach mom to let her know. I figured they'd be early anyway.

Now this was all before 9-11 when you could actually walk out to meet the folks coming off the plane. I arrived about an hour early and went up to the second floor and watched them below as they were watching for me to come off the plane.

Arcata is a small airport with small aircrafts. As the plane that I was supposed to be on landed, I watched as mom and Margie stood at the gate (on the same level as the plane was) looking for me.

I thought, "This must be how it is in Heaven! Being able to see your loved ones, but they can't see you!"

As the last passenger exited the plane, I decided I had better get down there and greet them. I walked up behind them and overheard them saying, "Where is Kay?"

I said, "Are you all waiting for someone?" They never even looked back at me as mom responded to my question.

"Yes we are, my daughter Kay."

"Hum," I said, "Maybe I can help you!" That is when they turned to the familiar voice. We all laughed and hugged as I told them about my change of flight. Mom swatted me and called me a nut. Imagine that! That was kind of like the pot calling the kettle black!

Now that mom and dad are in Heaven, I like to *think* that once in awhile God allows them to peek through the windows of Heaven just to see how we are doing.

Mom is now up there watching me watch for Jesus to come take me where she and dad are. And I'm ready to go.

Alright, like Paul Harvey, let's get back to the rest of the story!

It was only a few months until the General Assembly and I was anxious to hear if Brother Biggers was indeed going to retire. After all, I needed time to get my ducks in a row. I balked against God because I still didn't want to leave. But He never let up, or gave up on me.

My friend, Ralph was conducting a revival in Willow Creek and called and asked if I would come. Willow Creek is only twelve miles from Hoopa. I told him yes, I'd come straight from work and I would be a little late.

I got there just as he was beginning to sing and preach. He didn't have a clue about the battle that was going on between me and God. Since he had moved down to southern California, I had not seen, or spoken to him in over a year.

Well, let's just say that God had my number that night! Everyone else could have left the building because that message was just for me. He hit the nail on the head and drove it home!

At the close of his message, he invited us to kneel and pray. The church was crowded, and I was seated in the back. So I knelt at the folding-type metal chair that I had been sitting in. God had spoken to me, and now I was going to speak to Him. This time it was going to be different, a lot different!

My spirit, will and self had been melted. That night I climbed onto the Potters wheel and surrendered to *His* will. My attitude was as different as day and night.

I told God that I would go anywhere and do anything He wanted me to do. I even told Him if He wanted me to go to Africa, I'd go! He assured me that was not where He wanted me to go. It started with an A, but it was not Africa. Shew, was I ever relieved about that!

By the time we finished conversing, there was a puddle of tears in that metal chair. And it was at that point that there was no turning back for me. When I surrendered to God that night, it was a done deal! I'd be a servant on wheels! I'd just wait to hear from Brother Biggers. I knew in my spirit that he would not be retiring, at least not for another year.

After the General Assembly concluded, Brother Biggers called to tell me that Brother Tomlinson had reappointed him back to Arkansas for another year.

A month had gone by since that revival meeting where I had surrendered my all to God. The devil had tried to make me second guess what I was feeling. Note* if we are not careful, we will allow time and circumstances to cause us to go back on what we said we would do.

My heart was in my throat. I had made God a promise that if He would give me *twelve* revivals (He gave me *seventeen*!) and if He would send Brother Biggers back to Arkansas, (and He did!) I would move.

Brother Biggers asked, "Are you willing to come and be the State Evangelist and C.P.M.A. Secretary for the state of Arkansas?" Well, what could I say?

I finally found my voice and replied, "I need two months to pay off some bills and also give my notice at work." He agreed to the arrangement and said he'd see me in November.

One of the hardest things I had to do, was to tell my three bosses that I was quitting. I remember well asking to speak to them in the office. I him-hawed around and finally said, "I am giving you all a two month notice, I will be leaving." Sometimes silence can be very loud! "Leaving? Where?" they asked.

This was the hard part. "Well," I took a deep breath. "I am moving to Arkansas to Evangelize." There! I had said it! I looked into their faces of disbelief. I had pulled so many jokes at work, who could blame them if they didn't believe me at first?

When they saw I was serious, and determined, they accepted it. Pritchard, Boyd and Joyce. They had become like family and this was very hard on me. And besides, I really liked working there. There was never a dull moment for sure!

They threw me a party. I love a party! It was November 1978 and they presented me with a hard-shell suitcase. I carried that suitcase for years, and miles and miles! It was very sentimental to me. I felt like I was carrying a piece of them around with me.

I always enjoyed my trips back to Hoopa. Jordan's Shopping Center was always on my list of first to go see! Thirty something years later, every once in a while, I still dream I am working there.

CHAPTER 4
PACKING UP IS HARD TO DO

Time flew by. Before I knew it, I was packed up for Arkansas! It was November 18, 1978. That was Molly's birthday. I would soon discover that it was also another ladies birthday. Melba McIntosh and I would become very good friends.

Since I could not take my dog with me and evangelize, I asked mom if she would take care of her for me. With tears running down her face, she said she would.

The next year, mom ran over Skeeter and killed her! This is *not* how I meant for mom to "take care of her"! Of course it was an accident. Skeeter had a bad habit of getting behind the wheel of a car. Margie had a dog named Suki. After that happened, Margie kept Suki away from mom for a long time! Not really.

I would like to tell you that I was very spiritual on that 2,300 mile drive, but I wasn't. My insides were crying out, "I want my mama!" And I could only imagine what she was doing.

I turned on the radio to listen to the news. I couldn't believe what they were saying! A man named Jim Jones had seduced over a thousand people to leave the United States and follow him to Guyana.

The newscaster said 909 people of the Peoples Temple in Jonestown, Guyana had drunk cyanide poisoning in an event termed "revolutionary suicide". There were a total of 918 dead before it was all over.

I couldn't believe it! I told God, "Well, this is a fine thing! You bring me out here to preach the Gospel for you, and now a so-called minister misleads over nine-hundred people, and now they are all dead!"

I only hoped that the folks in Arkansas wouldn't think I was like him! Wow! The things the devil puts in our head.

A friend of mine, Connie, came to Arkansas with me. After a while she felt led to go back to California. In fact, she went back and became the pastor of the Hoopa Church of God of Prophecy.

My first stop in Arkansas was my grannies! It was close to Thanksgiving and I was going to spend my first Thanksgiving away from my mom, dad, Rick and Margie. But, I was with my granny, aunts, uncles, and a host of cousins. I was content.

Besides, mom and dad were coming out the next month for Christmas! Since I was driving a little two-door, hatchback Toyota, they would be bringing my stuff back with them when they came.

I had not even been in Arkansas a week when mom called with bad news. Someone had broken into my house in Hoopa and stole a lot of things. I remember one of the items they stole was a brand new, still in the box, Mr. Coffee Pot Coffee Maker.

They took a lot of stuff. I got hurt, then I got mad! I asked God why did He let them do that? After all, I was out just trying to do His will!

Why do we automatically think, that just because we are serving the Lord, and doing the best for Him that we can, that we will never encounter hardships? That is so totally wrong!

Job is the greatest example of a perfect man, a man who was upright. A man who feared God. Yet, in one day everything was taken from him. Even his ten children. The Bible tells us that in all this, Job did not sin. Job 13:15 tells us that Job said, "Though he slay me, yet will I trust in him:" Wow!

Years ago I came to the conclusion, if God allowed this to happen to Job, and later on allowed much worse to happen to His only son, Jesus...who was I to think that I would leave this world never having a care?

Never having any troubles or trials. Just skipping through life singing *"Que Sera, Sera"* with Doris Day! Well, life is not like that is it?

So after I got alone with God and prayed, as we say, prayed through, I was alright. Jesus tells us in John 16:33, "These things I have spoken unto you, that in me ye might have peace. In the world ye shall have tribulation: but be of good cheer; I have overcome the world." Thank God that He overcame, and so can you and I!

I came to realize that the stuff that they stole was just that, *stuff*! Stuff can be replaced. I now own a Bunn Coffee Pot. It makes coffee so much faster than the one stolen!

I know what it is like to wonder where is my next meal coming from. I remember sitting in Kentucky Fried Chicken sopping a few biscuits in a bowl of their brown gravy. Why didn't I have chicken with it? Because I did not have the money for chicken. But back then, you could get their biscuits for a quarter each!

I've got to tell this story about my wonderful friends, Bob and Maryann Davis. From the very first time we met in 1978, we bonded like family. They were like a brother and sister to me. Oh my lands, the fun we have had!

Marilyn and Missy were their two little girls. Jena would soon be on the way. Look out world! Lol

Anyway, by the early 1980's, I would stay with them when I was not in revival. That wasn't very often. Back in the day it was not unusual to be gone in revivals three weeks out of the month. And sometimes I stayed with my granny in-between revivals.

One day I was getting packed up to go to a revival somewhere in Oklahoma. Bob had Maryann to ask me if I had enough money. I wouldn't ever let them know if I was in need of money. I was very prideful and self-sufficient.

Maryann asked me if I had enough money for the trip. I said yes, I had money. I didn't tell her I only had ten dollars. My thinking was this; ten dollars to eat with and I had a full tank of gas in my Toyota that would take me all the way to the revival. And, I would fill up with gas to come home with the money I received from the revival.

Bob was suspicious and asked exactly how much money did I have? I said I had enough. He asked Maryann to give me their Texaco credit card. I said, "No way am I taking that card!"

But they wouldn't have it any other way. Just to satisfy them, I took it and told them that I would take it, but I would *not* use it. Boy, was I glad that was over with!

To my surprise, at the end of the revival, the church gave me a check instead of cash. Back then, it was more common to pay the evangelist via cash.

Well, I was in a pickle. How was I going to fill my car up with gas now? I was too proud to let the pastor know I didn't have any money. At that time, I didn't even own a credit card. And even if the gas station would take a personal check, I didn't have enough money in my account to cover it. And I don't believe in writing hot checks.

Finally it dawned on me, the Texaco credit card the Davis's gave me! Yippee! I may have been down, but I wasn't out! I put ten dollars in my tank, believe it or not, that filled my little tank up. Of course the gas was only $1.25 a gallon then.

I took the card in (you didn't pay at the pump then) and the man ran it through his machine. He gave it back to me and said, "That card is expired." I thought, "Expired? And Bob *made* me take it!"

I didn't flinch. I told him that I would go to the car and that I would be right back. Well, once I was in the car I thought, "Why did I come out here? Is money going to mysteriously appear?"

It was at that moment I could identify with what Spencer Tracy once said; "There were times my pants were so thin I could sit on a dime and tell if it was heads or tails." Now that's going some! Sometimes it's hard to have *a happy face* isn't it?

I sat in the car and I prayed. "Lord, what on earth am I going to do? I know what I'm going to do when I see Bob. I'm going to give him *back* his sorry *expired* credit card!"

I prayed and asked the Lord to help me. All of a sudden I remembered mom giving me a ten dollar bill. She said, "Stick this away somewhere and only use it for an emergency."

Well, if this wasn't an emergency, I didn't know what was! Now, where did I put that ten dollars? I searched all through my purse, not there. Where did I put it? Finally, I found it wrapped in a Kleenex on the bottom of my ash tray. It was weathered pretty badly, but still in one piece. Thank you Jesus and thank you mama!

I paid for the gas and was on my way. I couldn't wait to get rid of that credit card! On the way home, I began to laugh at the whole situation.

I knew they *didn't* know the card was expired. That thought never crossed my mind. They are not that kind of people. They would give you their last meal, that is if it wasn't expired! I'm sorry, I couldn't help myself.

When I arrived home that evening I gave them the card back without saying anything. They said, "Why don't you keep that card. We would feel a lot better if you had it for emergencies."

I said, "Oh I had an emergency alright. The church paid me with a check and I didn't have enough cash to fill the car up."

"Great!" they said. "So you did need the credit card. See, that's even more reason right there for you to carry that card with you!"

I couldn't keep it in any longer. I said, "No, I don't want that card."

"Yes, you keep that card!" they insisted.

"No, I don't want that card because, because its EXPIRED!" I began to laugh as they looked at the date to see if I was just kidding. When they realized it was indeed expired, they wanted to know how I was able to get the gas. I told them about mom's emergency money.

You see, we haven't always had money jingling in our pockets, or heard meat frying in the pan. But we've always had fun along this road, hand in hand with Jesus!

God has always taken care of me. I have funny stories to tell, but I don't have gloomy stories to remember. Oh yes, I've had my share of troubles, a lot of them I've brought on all by myself. But as David stated in Ps 37:25 "…yet have I not seen the righteous forsaken, nor his seed begging bread." Can I get an amen?

There was a time that I wondered how I was going to buy some shampoo and hairspray. I never said anything to anyone, except I told God about it. I just knew He didn't want me going around in revivals with fly-a-way hair!

The next day I went to get the mail, and there was a package from my sweet friend, Melba McIntosh! Melba has been a wonderful friend to me through these many years. She and her husband, Gene, have been there for me through thick and thin. They stood by me during the deaths of mom and dad.

Anyway, I opened the box and it was packed with all kinds of hair care. I hollered, "Thank you Jesus, and Melba!" Once again, God came through for me.

You see, if you never go through a test, you'll never have great testimonies like these! Lol

Some folks today want to be guaranteed a certain amount before they go. Like I said earlier, you can't bargain with God! I have never told a pastor that I had to be promised a certain amount of money before I came for revival. There were sometimes I wished I had! No, just kidding... sort of.

If God calls you, He will go with you. That is not to say that you will never have trials or tribulations. But if God is in it, you can't lose!

Throughout these thirty-five years of full-time ministry, I can truthfully say that God has never let me down. He is so great! At different times He has laid on a churches heart, or an individual's heart to send me a check. And guess what? It was just in time.

I believe that God is always on time, but sometimes He scares me to death! Sometimes He waits until it's just in the nick of time. Wow! That will keep you on your knees. But hey, that makes life that much more interesting!

I finally came to the place in my life that I relaxed and said, "You know God, I'm Your's and You're mine. I love You and You love me. I'm going to try not to worry or fret. You care for the sparrows, and You care for me!"

So God and I have an understanding, we love each other and we love people! Folks don't care how much you know until they know how much you care!

All of this down here will pass away, its just stuff. But souls, that is the most important of all! So many times my heart has cried out, "Lord, give me souls, lest I die!"

When we leave this world, we will not take anything with us. Have you ever seen a trailer hitch on the back of a hearse? No! Why? Because, you can't take it with you when you go.

Runing through the fire with souls in my hands!

And others save with fear, pulling them out of the fire; Jude 23

We need to pull others from the fire as stated in Jude 23.

CHAPTER 5
PLEASE, NO MORE CHICKEN NOODLE SOUP

I held my very first revival as State Evangelist at Des Arc, Arkansas! The pastors were Clay and Bonnie Frost. I fell in love with them and their five children right away. Their oldest son, Randy was already married, and so was their oldest daughter, Kathy. So they still had three kids left at home, Robin, Jennifer and Duane. Although, Robin was getting ready to marry.

We had a great revival and I made some lifelong friends. In years to come as I would travel the state, sometimes I stayed with Frances and Jerry Owen. They have two children, Tim and Sherry. Sherry was always so kind to let me have her bedroom when I stayed with them. So kind? She charged me rent! Not really, but it was an on going joke.

You want to talk about a cook, that Frances can cook! Good ole southern style. And her tea is fantastic! If you are ever in Des Arc, just drop by and see for yourself. Tell her Kay sent ya!

Thanksgiving and Christmas flew by faster than I had wanted it to. Mom and dad had left to go back to Hoopa where Margie and Rick were. I was going to begin my next revival in Arkansas.

I was beginning to form close friendships with many of the church folks. I was getting less nervous all the time and feeling more and more like this was really what God wanted me to do.

Then it happened. An ice storm. It was the first part of January 1979. I had lived here less than two months. The ice covered the state. A pastor called and needed to cancel the revival. That was fine with me. I couldn't get out of my driveway anyway.

As if that wasn't bad enough, six days later the Lord allowed yet another ice storm! This one worse than the first. Another pastor called and canceled revival, then another. Well, I was not prepared for this! Especially financially. Fifty dollars wasn't going to go very far this month.

I began to worry. I prayed pitiful prayers to God. Trust me, its much better to pray *powerful* prayers! I was so worried about my car payment, the rent, the light bill and electricity bill. Food was running low as well. And with no revivals, how was I to make it?

I got aggravated and told the Lord, "Did you bring me out here to die?! Was this all a joke? Look at me, I'm wrapped up like an Eskimo just to keep from running the heat! This trailer is so drafty; I see dollar bills blowing right out the corners of the walls!"

Looking back, I must have sounded a lot like the Children of Israel complaining to Moses! "Did you bring us out to the desert to die?"

The thought crossed my mind to call mom and dad to help me make my car payment. But I said, "No! I'll not do it! They did not call me out here God, You did. If you don't help me, well, then I'll just starve to death. I'm not calling them, and I'm not calling Brother Biggers either."

I was so eaten up with pride. I think all of Arkansas had to suffer these two ice storms just for God to teach me a lesson. And for that, I apologize. For every pound I weighed, there was a pound of pride that went with it!

I knew my car payment was due in two weeks. I always believed in getting it in a little before the due date. And I was a stickler for paying my bills. My credit report was, and still is A+ and I didn't want it ruined.

One day I knelt beside my bed and told God I was desperate to get that car payment in the mail. I told Him the make and model of the car, the color and even the license plate number! I meant business. I know God was laughing at me because He could see the big picture. All I could see was ice and snow. Oh yes, snow fell on top of the ice, then melted a little bit, then froze to ice. Wonderful!

I was getting hungry and money was getting low. There was a Safeway store right down from where I lived. I had a few dollars left, so I went grocery shopping. The special of the week was *Campbell's Chicken Noodle Soup*, five cans for a dollar! Whoo-hoo! I bought four dollars worth, twenty cans.

I had pretty much eaten everything else in the house, so I started on the soup. Soup Monday, soup Tuesday, soup Wednesday and soup Thursday. You get the picture.

Once again I thought of the Children of Israel when they complained about their food. They wanted something different. So God rained down so much quail that it made them sick. The Bible says it came out their nostrils! (Numbers 11:20) Yuck! I felt like if I ate another can of that chicken noodle soup, noodles would be coming out of mine!

I was hungry for some meat! Something I could sink my teeth into. You could go blind eating chicken noodle soup, just by trying to find the chicken!

Brother Elvie Underwood was the pastor at Searcy. He called one day and asked if he could bring me some chicken and dressing. Said he had made too much. My pride was diminishing, a little. I said, "Well, only if you have it to spare."

Never having eaten his cooking before, I wondered just how good it would be. But hey, I was getting desperate! He knocked on the door, I opened it and there he stood with that big smile on his face. I jerked him into the house...not really. He came in and sat the dish on the stove. It was still hot from the oven!

I lifted up the corner of the foil and soon the kitchen was filled with the wonderful aroma of homemade chicken and dressing! He stood there talking about how bad the ice was and when it would ever thaw out enough to have church again.

The aroma was getting to me. I wanted to wait for him to leave before I dug into it. Because I knew when I began to dig into it, there would be no stopping me! It was not going to be a pretty picture. I loved Brother Underwood like a grandpa, but I thought he'd never leave!

As soon as he was out the door, I tore into that pan of food. It was the very best chicken and dressing I had ever eaten in my life! He was a great cook! I never thought about tomorrow as I ate the whole thing. Gracious, it was good!

The menu for the next day was more chicken noodle soup. "Please God, I've had enough already!" My prayers were beginning to be a little more humble. I began to tell God how much I loved Him and that I just knew He was going to see me through. And at night I would dream about Brother Underwood's chicken and dressing!

The stockpile of soup was beginning to get low. But I didn't care, I was sick of it! About that time the phone rang. I thought it was probably another pastor calling to cancel the next revival. It was a pastor, but he wasn't calling to cancel. It was Brother and Sister Frost. Bonnie and Clay talked for a little while and then told me why they *really* had called.

"We figured your revivals had been canceled and wondered if you would like to come and spend some time with us? There is no need of you burning your heat when you can be enjoying ours!" they said.

Wow! Heat and food! What else could a gal ask for? I was jumping up and down on the inside but tried to remain calm in my voice. I didn't want them to think I was about to starve. Hey wait a minute! I was about to starve!

So as not to sound desperate, I replied. "Well, revivals are slow. If you are sure it won't be an inconvenience, I don't want to be an inconvenience..."

What on earth was I doing? God was making a way, and I was about to mess it up with foolish pride!

They pursued, "You might as well come on. The kids have been asking about you and we will have a blast!" I thought about what a great cook Bonnie was and how much fun me and their kids had playing board games.

"Alright, I'll be glad to come. It will be nice to get out of this trailer for a few days. I heard on the news that the roads are getting a lot better for traveling." I was getting excited!

It is only thirty miles from Searcy to Des Arc. It probably took me all of ten minutes to pack and hit the road! I was there in time for supper, and what a supper it was! I ate like it was the last supper. After all, I was only twenty-three years old and I needed my strength!

I never spoke of my situation to them while I was there. I acted like I had money in my pocket and food in my pantry. It wasn't necessary to bring all my woes on them.

They were able to have church that Wednesday night. They asked me to preach, and then received a love offering for me. Wow! Gas money!

At the close of the service, Brother Frost said, "Sister Kay, the church at Des Arc loves you and we wanted to show our love to you." At that moment, men began to carry boxes and bags of groceries to the front pew where I was sitting. So many groceries!

I was so humbled and at the same time, ashamed. Ashamed of how I had thought God had forsaken me. Ashamed for not trusting Him the way I should have. Tears trickled down my face as I tried to thank the church.

When it was time to leave and go back to Searcy, it was hard to fit all those groceries in the car! God had showed up and showed out. He showed me that He never intended to let His little girl starve, or go without. It was a test, a test of trust and love.

When I got home, I unloaded all those groceries and guess what? There was not one can of chicken noodle soup! Hallelujah! Even to this day, I do not care for that soup. Oh, I'd eat it if I had too.

God had come through for me! But I was still concerned about that car payment. It needed to be in the mail the next day! I opened my mail and there it was! Brother Biggers had sent me a check from the state. He had written, "I suppose some of your revivals have been canceled due to all this ice. Here is a little something to tie you over until your revivals pick back up again."

You guessed it. The check was enough to pay my tithes, make the car payment, and get me to the next revival! God was watching out for me then, just like He is watching out for me now… thirty-five years later in full-time ministry!

Happiness keeps you sweet. Trials keep you strong. Sorrows keep you human. Failure keeps you humble, and God keeps you going! – Unknown

"Just Us Chickens!"
May 1955

CHAPTER 6
FAMILY, TOGETHER AGAIN!

In May of 1988 my sister, Margie and I, as well as two of our friends, Michele and Susan, took a vacation to Hawaii! Three months prior, I had been in a bad storm. Large hail had beat my Camry up pretty bad.

The insurance company paid for the damage. Instead of having it fixed, I decided to drive a dimpled up car and go to Hawaii. That was the only way I could afford the trip. I'd walk by my car and put my finger in one of the dents and move it from dent to dent and say, "Aloha, Aloha, Aloha!"

We went and had a wonderful time! Oahu was absolutely beautiful! We saw as many things as we could in the time we had. Then we flew over to Maui. The most popular shirt there was, "Here today, gone to Maui!" It was great.

Vacations are always over sooner than you want them to be, aren't they? I know this one was. Now it was time to get back to Arkansas and prepare for our annual State Convention.

The Convention ended July 17, 1988. My Godparents, Charlie and Wilma Gentle were in attendance, along with their six-year old granddaughter, Sandy.

The four of us had made plans to go to the Memphis zoo as soon as the convention was over. We had a great time. I even rode a camel with Sandy!

It was about midnight when I got back to Hope. I was staying with my friends, the Davis's. I quietly came in and went straight to my bedroom. Maryann had left a note on my bed that read, "Wake me when you come in. It doesn't matter how late it is, wake me." Again, back then, there were no cell phones.

I knew something was wrong. I'll never forget the seriousness in their voice. They told me that Margie had been in a really bad accident. I stood there unable to move as I asked them how bad it was. Maryann looked at Bob, then back at me and told me it was really, really bad.

Margie, mom and dad were two-thousand-three-hundred miles away from me. Rick and I were both living in Arkansas, about two-hundred miles apart. I never felt so far away as I did that night.

I began calling the hospital in Arcata, California. I finally was able to speak to mama. She and dad were there waiting for Margie to come out of surgery. It didn't sound good at all.

I caught a flight out the next day. That was a long flight, not knowing what I would hear when I got there. What if they told me she had died? I had just spent a week with her in Hawaii and all the fun times flooded my mind. I couldn't lose her, I just couldn't!

I had a window seat and thought I might be able to prop up against it and get some sleep. I had been awake all night packing, and then driving to Duncan, Oklahoma, where my friend, Linda Beal drove me to OKC airport. Linda also took care of my car while I was gone.

But sleep was far from me. When the thoughts of losing Margie would hit me, tears would fill my eyes as I'd turn and look out the window of that big airplane.

The accident had happened Sunday evening after church. Now the plane was touching ground in Arcata, California Monday evening. Our friend Molly Cotton had come to pick me up. What a relief it was when she told me, "Margie is out of surgery and is stable!"

"Thank God! Now just get me to the hospital as fast as you can," I replied.

Margie had been in surgery for thirteen hours! She was being held together by rods, plates, pins, screws and wire. But mostly by the hands of God almighty!

I knew Margie had been in a wreck, but didn't know any details. All I really knew is that Margie and Molly's daughter, Cathy were going down to the river Sunday evening after church to go swimming. When I arrived at the hospital mom and dad filled me in.

Margie and Cathy were in Margie's little blue Toyota pickup less than two miles from mom and dad's. They were going around a curve and was met by a Honda Civic on Margie's side of the road going about 85 MPH. He hit Margie on the drivers side.

Cathy's only injuries were her knees, they hit hard into the dash. Margie had major problems. She was stuck in the truck as the door was caved in and wouldn't open.

Cathy got a ride to mom and dads. Her mother, Molly was at the house as well. Cathy burst through the door and said, "Margie's hurt!" Mom immediately thought Margie had drowned. They rushed to the scene. The paramedics were there trying to free Margie from the vehicle.

They were trying with all of their might with the *jaws of life*. Then the jaws of life broke. Our dad walked up (all 6'2 of himself!) and said, "Stand aside boys, this is my daughter."

He reached under the truck and picked up a long rod/axle looking thing (I do not know all the technical names of car parts) and broke the door loose. He must have looked like walking tall to those guys!

Both of Margie's ankles were crushed, one was laying on the calf of her leg while the other one was twisted up in the brake and clutch. Margie remembers none of this, which is a blessing.

She was screaming in pain. Daddy said, "Margie, this is your daddy. We are going to get you to the hospital. I need you to settle down." Margie calmed down as dad gave way to the paramedics. He had done his job, now it was time for them to do theirs.

Boyd Jury was on the scene and knew the gearshift was in the way. Since it was a five-speed, the gearshift was on the floor. Boyd's adrenaline helped him to bend the gearshift to the floor so they could take Margie's legs and lay them in the passenger's seat. You may think this is hard to believe, especially since the gearshift was made of steel, but it is the truth. Boyd did for Margie like he would have done for his own daughter, Bonnie.

Mom found out that they were going to air-lift Margie to Arcata, California. So mom, Molly and Cathy got in the car and began the fifty mile drive over two mountains to the hospital in Arcata.

Since they were still working on Margie, trying to free her from the vehicle, they were able to beat the helicopter to the hospital. Mom was standing outside where the helicopter was going to land. One of the hospital staff came out and told mom, "Ma'am, you can't stand here, you must wait inside."

Now mom always obeyed rules, but this was her daughter and she wasn't going to budge. Mom replied, "That is my daughter in that helicopter, and I am not hurting anything by standing here out of the way. I *will* wait here." The lady backed off.

They air-lifted her to the nearest hospital in Arcata, where she underwent many hours of emergency surgery. The doctor was a Christian man. He described the bones in her ankles as "broken up granola bars". He put the pieces together as best he could with pins. At one point he thought he might have to amputate both ankles.

When I first saw Margie, I didn't recognize her because her face was so swollen. We would find out later that her chin was cracked. When she saw me, it must have scared her, thinking she was going to die! Why else would her sister from Arkansas be there? In fact, the first words out of her mouth were, "What are you doing here?" I said, "Oh,

I don't know. My little sister gets in a wreck and I fly out to see her!"

They said she would be in there for four to six weeks. But praise be to God, she was out in only two! We never left her side, and neither did God! The staff was amazed at her progress. We found out later that all the churches in Hoopa had prayer for Margie that Sunday evening as she was in surgery.

Mom was worried about how she was going to tell Margie about the young man who was driving the other car. He was drunk and had died at the scene. When mom told her, Margie only expressed sympathy for the young man's family.

Our brother, Rick, was able to get a flight out on Tuesday. So we all helped nurse Margie back to health. She was bedridden for awhile. She progressed to the wheelchair, then the walker, then the crutches, and then the cane. After months of therapy, she was walking with the help of God.

If anyone had a right (or an excuse) to stay home from church, Margie did. But the very first Sunday she was home, she wanted to be in church. They rolled her up to the piano in the wheelchair and with both of her legs in casts, she played for song service. Now that's dedication! It doesn't take much to get some folks to stay home on a Sunday morning. Where's my Amen sign?

I had stayed as long as I could and after three weeks I flew back to Arkansas. I will always be thankful to Larry Lowry for making the arrangements for me to fly out to my sister, and always thankful to the good people of Arkansas for funding it.

Margie would face several more surgeries in the following months. In one surgery, they had to cut the pointy part off of her hip bone and place it in her ankle. That's because there was not enough ankle bone left to support her.

It's amazing to me what God and the doctors can do! I also find it humorous that Margie is walking around on her hip bone!

All of this happened just before her twenty-eighth birthday. Here it is twenty-five years later and she is still walking with the Lord. The accident took its toll on her, leaving her with a limp and with good ole arthritis. But not much slows her down. She has been in banking most of her life.

In July 1990, Margie moved to Hope, Arkansas. It was always mom and dads dream to move back home to Harrisburg, Arkansas. Dad had a logging accident in 1989 and was forced to take an early retirement.

They sold their house in Hoopa and in September of 1990, some twenty-eight years later, all the kids grown, they packed up and moved back *"home"* to Harrisburg, Arkansas. Once more, the family was all together again!

I will always be thankful to God for allowing mom and dad to move closer to me. I never dreamed that six years and three months later, mom would die of lymphoma cancer.

One of the saddest days of my life was when I found out mama only had about six months to live. On a Wednesday night, we all stood around mama's bed as we said goodbye to her. It was January 22, 1997 the day after her 65th birthday.

Rick was in route from California (he had moved to L.A.) trying to get there before she passed. He and his wife had just had a baby boy, Jesse, three weeks earlier. Unfortunately, mama left us forty-five minutes before he could get there. Life would never be the same again, never!

I wrote this poem on the fourteenth year anniversary of her death:

Mom, you went to be with Jesus 14 years ago today.
Nothing, I mean NOTHING has ever been the same.

You were the life of the party at every event,
You made everyone feel loved wherever you went.
Your laughter and smile I'll never forget,
You were so funny, so full of wit!
I miss you more each and every day,
Still struggle with why you went away.
No longer do you lay under that sod,
You're with Jesus, just praising our God.
                                  - Kay Osban 1-22-11

My Parents, Jessie & Willie Osban

Parents

    I want to share some more about my parents. I preached my dad's funeral October 9, 2011. Here are just some of the things I said:

    Dad was a real character. He enjoyed having fun. If he and mom had company in the evening hours, when he was ready to go to bed, he would say, "If y'all are waiting up for me, I believe I feel better."

He'd tell folks that he left Arkansas on account of his belief; he got to believing other peoples chickens were his.

He loved to play the guitar. He would sing "Frankie and Johnny".

Dad had backslidden back in the 70's. We had all prayed fervently for him to be restored back to the Lord.

Dad always kept his word. Back in 1994 mom had a huge mass in her stomach and had to have it removed. We were all waiting for the doctor to come out and give us the results.

They told us they had removed a twenty-seven pound tumor from her stomach! And they said mom was going to be alright.

The next Sunday, January 17, 1994, Margie was here at the Harrisburg church. She was in the middle of singing a special song when she noticed daddy get up and begin to walk down the aisle to the front. When he got to the altar, he knelt down. Margie was thinking, "What is he doing? Has he lost something at the altar?"

The answer to that question is *yes*, but that morning he found what he had lost, he found Jesus!

We found out later that he had told the Lord that he would get saved and serve him the rest of his life if he let Jessie live through that surgery. The Lord let mom live and dad kept his word; I'll serve you Lord until the day I die. He has kept his word right up to this day.

I asked him in the hospital if everything was alright with him and Jesus, and he gave a resounding YES!

Dad was fortunate enough to have loved two wives, our mom, Jessie and for the past 9 years, Ruth.

Ruth, you were good for dad, and dad was good for you. He loved you, and you loved him. He would probably not have lived to be nearly eighty-one-years old had he not found someone else to love and have companionship with.

You two had so much fun when it came time to can all the goodies from your garden. No telling how many hundreds of jars of salsa, corn, peaches, tomatoes, vegetable soup, pickles and stewed deer you guys canned together.

Every time I would visit, just as I was getting ready to leave, dad would say, "Come on Kay, I know you want to raid my pantry." He'd take me where they had stacked all the canned goods and begin to load me up.

Rick, you were his buddy, fishing together, gardening together, canning together and going to church together. So many times while you guys were out fishing, he would tell you how glad he was that you had moved back here. In California, you guys were even partners in cutting timber together.

One day you got a tree on top of you. Dad got so nervous; he jumped up on the tree that you were under. You managed to squeeze out enough breath to say, "Hey dad, will you lighten the load?" He then jumped down and cut the tree off of you.

Dad, the Lumberjack!

For the past several years you two were together almost everyday. You called him your best friend and hero. The man who made you the man you are today. You're going to miss him a lot.

Margie, Rick was his buddy, but you were his baby! He was so proud of you. He loved to hear you play the piano more than anything. He loved it so much, that he bought you a brand new Baldwin piano when you graduated from high school.

When I graduated, I got a Bible. What's wrong with this picture? Well, she went on to become a great piano player and I've taken the Bible across the United States. I guess the moral of this story is "Be careful what you get your kids for graduation!" I think they got Rick a new radiator, and he's been blowing off steam ever since!

Margie, he loved it every time you got to come and visit. Seems like the Lord worked it out for you to come several times this year. He was proud of the parent you had become to Quinton. He said you raised a polite boy. His eyes would light up when you walked in the room.

The last time I spoke with him on the phone, I told him it was your birthday. He immediately told one of the nurses, "Hey, today is my daughters birthday!" He said it with so much joy in his voice. He loved you for the lady you have become.

To the grandchildren, Dad loved to pick at kids, especially his grandkids. He loved it when Rick's kids would drop in and he would offer them a Pepsi or a candy bar. He loved making things for them.

He told me that when he was making Sara a dresser for her birthday, he'd be in the backyard working on it and Sara would come back there and say, "Grandpa, what are you making?" Daddy would just smile. We all have something in our house that daddy made, and it was made with love!

Before he'd get off the phone with Margie, he'd always say, "Give that boy a whooping for me!" He was talking about Quinton.

A few years ago I held a revival here at the Harrisburg church. At the close of the last night, Brother Elliott ask if anyone had anything they would like to say.

Daddy spoke up and said how much he enjoyed the revival. Then he broke down crying and said, "She is a good person and we need to pray for her as she travels everywhere preaching revivals." It took me off guard. But once again, it just showed how tender daddy's heart was. His bark really was a lot worse than his bite.

He would call Margie and me every Saturday. Once when he called, he had a head cold. Before we hung up, I told him that I would be praying for him to be healed. He responded, "Well, I'll probably get well anyway." We are going to miss those calls!

About four months ago dad asked me when I was coming home. I told him it would be Christmas. He said, "Well, why don't you book some revivals this direction and we'll go fishing?" I laughed and said I'd see what I could do about that.

I thought Dad was trying to be my manager! I made a few calls and called him back and told him I'd see him the second week of November.

I'm not going to be able to do that. But as dad stepped over to the other side, I imagine Mom standing there with a golden fishing pole in her hand saying, "'Bout time you got here! Come on in, the fishing is great!"

FISHERMAN'S PRAYER
I pray that I may live to fish, until my dying day.
And when it comes to my last cast,
I then must humbly pray:
When in the Lord's great landing net,
And peacefully asleep,

That in His mercy I be judged
Good enough to keep!

This past Father's Day, I sat down and wrote this poem for daddy. After he read it, he told Margie that I had put it on a little thick!

A Tribute to My Dad!
My dad is a man's man!
He can make a deal by shaking your hand.
Dad has never stolen, he's not a crook.
But he'll bring you a mess of fish
He caught on a hook!
Everyone knows how dad likes to fish,
To catch the most and the biggest is his only wish.
Dad believes in keeping his word,
He'd tell you once, just hope that you heard!
When dad gives you his word, take it to the bank.
If ever he was late, it was because his boat sank!
He can pick a guitar clean,
But please, please don't ask him to sing!
He'll start with "Frankie & Johnny were Sweethearts"
By the time he is finished, the company departs.
He can build anything out of wood,
Cabinets, dressers, shelves... they are all good!
Yes sir! This man I call dad,
He's the best that this ole girl could ever have had!!!

By Kay Osban on Fathers Day, June 2011

CHAPTER 7
A MOUNTAIN TOP EXPERIENCE
(SUKI'S BREATH IS KILLING US!)

It was December 1987. I had driven from Arkansas to Hoopa, California, to spend Christmas with mom, dad and Margie.

A few days after Christmas, Margie and I set out to do our yearly tradition, to drive as far up the mountain that we could in the snow. I had a Camry, front wheel drive, and was so excited to see just how far up in the snow we could go.

Margie's dog, Suki went with us. Taking Suki along with us turned out to be a big mistake. The dog had bad breath, big time!

As we climbed the mountain in my car, we met skiers coming down. They were having so much fun, as were we. "Were" is the key word here people.

After a while, we began to notice that we weren't meeting anyone, or any other vehicles coming down the mountain. The snow was getting deeper!

Margie suggested that we turn around. But no! I wanted to see just how far up the mountain this Camry would take us! Picture it, a dirt mountain road with no guard rails! If one were to go over the cliff, one would probably never be found.

Now the only tire tracks being made in the snow, were being made by us. The temperature had dropped dramatically because we were at such a high elevation.

At one point, (I remember this very vividly) I gunned the car and we *flew* up on top of the snow. The car was now high centered on top of the snow. The tires were not touching the ground, so they were freewheeling!

I told Margie, "We are, we are..." (I could not think of the word *high centered*!) Margie completed the sentence for me, "We are stuck!" I said, "Yeah that too!"

We got out of the car into the cold and stretched the tire chains out on the ground. We then tried to put the chains on the tires, just to find out that the chains were too short! What can I say; my last car had smaller tires.

You must remember, back in the day there were *no cell phones*. And it was beginning to get dark.

We scrounged up what paper we could find, and tried to build a fire. But being the neat freak that I am, my trash bag in the car was pretty well empty. Couple that with the fact all the wood was wet... well, I think you get the picture.

Margie had our brother Rick's big ole video camera with us. You know, the great big VHS? AnyWho, we videoed each other telling our mom and dad goodbye. I have Margie on tape reading the 23rd Psalm, along with other verses from the Bible. She sounded so pitiful, sort of like she thought we might actually die up there.

Meanwhile, Suki was hyperventilating. She knew something was wrong and began to breathe harder and faster. With each breath she breathed, I gagged. Her breath was atrocious!

Joke: Political correctness. A man was talking about the difference between a dog's brain vs. a man's brain. An offended man said, "Wait a minute, you can't talk about a dog like that".

We began to get hungry. Then we began to starve. All I had in my car was red hot jawbreakers. I use to keep a supply of them in my car. If I got a little sleepy while driving, I'd pop one of them in my mouth, and I'd be wide awake.

We had visions of making sandwiches from the leftover turkey and then washing it down with one of mom's homemade pies. But, you guessed it; all we had were... jawbreakers!

Our mom and dad loved to watch, "*The Wheel of Fortune*". We began to pray that the puzzle would say, "Kay and Margie are stuck up on the mountain!"

Meanwhile back at the ranch, mom and dad were beginning to worry about us. Dad jumped in his truck and drove up the mountain as far as he could, then had to turn around and come back. I cannot even explain to you how worried mom was.

Dad called my ex-boss, Boyd Jury. He knew that Boyd had a 4-Wheel Drive truck. He explained the situation to him.

By now, mom had quite the gathering of supporters at the house. There was Molly Cotton, Joyce Jury, Eleanor Foust and Michele Lightner. Michele was an EMT, and decided to join dad and Boyd in this rescue. Suki's breath was getting worse!

Meanwhile, it's getting colder. I would only run the car for a few minutes, just long enough that we could get warm. I didn't want us to die of carbon monoxide. Heaven forbid we should do that!

We spotted headlights coming up the mountain. Could it be, please let it be, it was! It was Dad! Quickly I turned my flashers on. Then something happened that we didn't expect. The vehicle stopped, then began to go BACK down the mountain!

Margie and I jumped out into the cold and began waving our arms and yelling, "Help, help!" The other vehicle stopped. The door opened and out stepped Dad.

It was at this very moment that we realized we were *not* going to die of hypothermia. It was also at this very moment that we wondered if we would die at the hands of our dad. Really! You had to see the anger in his walk. You've seen the movie, "Walking Tall?" Well, he was, "Walking Mad Dad!"

You may be wondering why their truck stopped, then began to back down the hill. You'd have to know our dad's sense of humor to understand this.

When Dad saw my car, and he knew we were alright, he asked Boyd to act like they were going to leave us. When Dad would tell this story, he'd lean way back and laugh as he'd say, "You should have seen Margie and Kay jump out of that car with their arms a waving!"

Well, they were able to get us "low-centered" or "un-high-centered", or as Margie would say, "*unstuck!*"

On the way DOWN the mountain, we met the Highway Patrol coming UP the mountain. They stopped me. I rolled my window down and they asked, "Are you the Osban sisters?" I replied, "Yes sir". They said, "Well, now that we see that you all are alright, we will call off the helicopter search."

Now somehow I found that to be funny. Margie, on the other hand, didn't. She explained to me, "There are so many people in Hoopa that have scanners. By the time I go back to work tomorrow, this story will be all over the valley. How embarrassing!" I assured her that it wouldn't be *that* bad. At least not for me, as I would be leaving back to Arkansas! She didn't see the humor in it. Sometimes I just don't understand her.

When dad picked up his truck at Boyd's house, they called mom to let her know all was well. So when we walked in the house, mom was standing there with a flyswatter in her hand. She said, "Both of you, TO THE ROOM!" That always meant that we were going to get a whooping. Then she put the swatter down, and her arms up for a hug. All's well that ends well. At least that's what I say!

Hope, Arkansas, 2007 - Kay, Rick, Charlie, Wilma, Ruth, Dad & Margie

We all had a wonderful Thanksgiving together. My friend Lois came and helped cooked. We had lots of racks of ribs! Who says you have to have turkey on Thanksgiving?! Everyone enjoyed the food, especially Daddy!

Rick Turns 60!

CHAPTER 8
LET'S HAVE A REVIVAL!

I have enjoyed these years evangelizing for the Lord. I have ministered in twenty-seven states. I've been in every state, except Alaska and North Dakota. I've been the guest speaker at several Ladies Retreats and Conferences on State and National level.

I do Ladies Night Out, where ladies come together to relax, let their hair down and laugh awhile. Although I am not a member, I also speak at Red Hat Conventions Now that's fun! Mrs. Cookie Hays is the Queen.

Over the past thirty-five years there have been so many great revivals that I have been privileged to be a part of. I have only chosen a few to write about. God alone holds the record in Heaven of what has been accomplished down here on earth for Him. To God be all the glory forever and ever, amen!

Fayetteville, Arkansas

Fayetteville, Arkansas, was probably one of the scariest of all, weather wise that is. There was no room in the parsonage for me to stay. But there was a room in the back of the church that they had fixed up as a bedroom.

That night, a terrible thunderstorm came in. It was lightning, it rained, it thundered and the wind blew mightily. I didn't know if the storm would bust the window out or tear the roof off! There were times I was sure I would not live to see the next day. But, I did! The pastor acted like it was nothing. Being from California, I was not use to this weather at all.

Have you ever been sound asleep and a bolt of lightning hits right outside your window? It will make you holler hi-de-ho! There is just nothing like Arkansas and Oklahoma weather. You may go to sleep in one town and wake up in another!

Then there was the revival at Solid Rock Ministries in Siloam Springs, Arkansas, with Pastor Dwayne Driggers. It was August 1997. It was only scheduled for a few nights. Don't you just love it when God messes with your schedule?

This is what was written up in the newspaper, *The Herald Leader*:

"REVIVAL FIRE FALLS AT SOLID ROCK MINISTRIES"

Revival began on Sunday morning August 24th. The presence of God was felt as the praise team led in worshipping the King of Kings. Sunday and Monday nights were no exception to the rule. God's Spirit was so strong, no one was worried about the time.

Then on Tuesday night it happened, all of Heaven opened and God poured His Spirit down in abundance. The praise team had led us into the presence of the Almighty. Then Pastor Dwayne Driggers began to exhort with a powerful unction.

About that time, one of the laymen ran to the front and exclaimed, "The Lord has just shown me a vision in which He was standing in the middle of a large body of water and He is bidding all of us to step in".

Evangelist Kay Osban read the words to a song, "I'm going to wade right in". At that time, the Holy Ghost flooded the place.

People began to get up off their pew and come to the front where the Water of the Spirit seemed to be the strongest. This went on for over an hour. Tongues and interpretations went forth.

A lady said her friend was laying down in the nursery because of severe pain from a swollen ovary. We all went back and gathered around her and prayed for her. Evangelist Osban said, "I want all the adults to stand back and let the children pray for her."

Seven small children knelt around her, laying their little hands on her while tears streamed down their faces as they fervently prayed. In a moment's time, the pain in her face was replaced with a smile as she got up and began to praise the Lord for healing her body.

Everyone began to walk towards the front of the church, but several were detained by the Spirit just outside the nursery door. Prayer one for another continued with shouts of joy and dancing in the Spirit.

Pastor Driggers proceeded to admonish everyone to flow in the stream that God had prepared for them that night.

Evangelist Osban spoke, "The Lord has instructed me to read Jeremiah 18:1-4. It tells of the potter's house and how one became married and was put back on the wheel and was made over again."

She continued, "The Lord has shown me a *human potter's wheel*. I want the Pastor and two other brethren to get into a circle.

Anyone desiring to be made over again, I want you to come forth and stand in the middle of this circle. Let this human potter's wheel turn you around and around as the Lord makes you over again as it seems good to Him."

Nearly 100% stood in line, waiting their turn on the potter's wheel. Many have said, "I've never seen anything like this before! The power of God was so strong that we could hardly stand up."

As some came out of the circle, they were slain in the Spirit. While one person was on the potter's wheel, the Lord healed him of a stomach ulcer and increased his eye sight.

There were people lying all over the floor. One man was out in the Spirit for over an hour. When he came to, he got up and stood by the pastor. A mighty wind from God knocked him back to the floor where he remained until three a.m., out in the Spirit.

At eleven, one gentleman tried to leave and when he stepped outside the door, he was slain on the ground by the power of God. The next night, the man who had been slain until three in the morning, shared with the congregation what the Lord had shown him while "out in the Spirit".

One lady had gone to the doctor a week before the revival started. He found a cyst the size of a lemon on her ovary. On the first night of revival she came forward for prayer.

The following Thursday she went back for another check up. The doctor asked her if she had had surgery because the cyst was gone and there was nothing left but a scar. To God be the glory! Revival fire continues to fall each night as the crowd increases.

All of this is backed up by the Scripture. Acts 2:17-18 says, "And it shall come to pass in the last days, saith God, I will pour out of my Spirit upon all flesh: and your sons and your daughters shall prophesy, and your young men shall see visions, and your old men shall dream dreams: And on my servants and on my handmaidens I will pour out in those days of my Spirit, and they shall prophesy."

That newspaper article caused many others to come to this Holy Ghost filled revival. If for no other reason, they came just to see the fire burn.

That reminds me of a joke I heard years ago about a church building burning to the ground. A neighbor came and stood beside the pastor as they watch this huge fire.

The pastor looked at him and said, "This is the first time I have ever seen you at church". The man replied, "Well Pastor, this is the first time your church has ever been on fire!"

Believe me when I tell you, Solid Rock Ministries was definitely on fire! It was a powerful revival that I shall never forget.

That was the first, and last time that God ever instructed me to have a *human potter's wheel*. It would have been easy for me in my next revival, to try to do that again. It would have failed because God was the one who orchestrated that one.

Too many times we think, "If God did it like that last week, surely He will do it like that this week." Not always. God is a God of diversity. Now don't you fall out with me over that statement. All that means is God can do whatever, however and wherever He pleases. We cannot put God in a box because He will not be boxed in.

You can only imagine in your mind's eye what it looked like seeing all those souls laying on the floor, slain in the Spirit of God! We call that, doing "carpet time."

I have been back to Dwayne and Jennifer's several times since that revival. I have found the very same God showing up in each and every service in a mighty way. In fact, I am scheduled to go there again this year.

June 28, 2009 Show and Tell

Once again I was preaching at Gentry, AR. with Dwayne Driggers as the pastor. Anyway, we had a great day in the Lord. That morning I preached on healing.

Right in the middle of my message, someone came and got the pastor. He was gone for a short time, then he came back in. He stopped my message (*on healing*) and said, "Folks, this is not staged or put on, but we have a lady in the foyer that is doubled over in pain and I need Sister Kay to come and pray for her."

So, I stopped my message on *"healing"* and went and prayed for her. On the way to her I thought to myself, "Lord, its all about You, and Your Word is true. Show Yourself strong."

She was in great pain; she was pale and holding her stomach. I prayed for her, she said she felt a little better. I told her we wanted total healing. We prayed again. I knew the second that God healed her, her arms went up in the air praising the Lord! Her color came back and she had a big smile on her face.

I came back to finish my message on healing and told them what *God* had done. Afterwards, two were saved, one for the very first time. Several were healed.

Later that day, Dwayne and I began to laugh as we thought about how that morning had been *Show and Tell*! I preached about healing, and *God* showed them what *He* could do!

I tell you God is so good, and He is true to His Word. If we will **ONLY BELIEVE**! That is what He told us to do, only believe.

January 1980

I was scheduled for a weekend revival in Trumann, Arkansas. The weather was cold, very cold. But the services were red hot with the power of God!

This revival was going really well. Souls were getting saved and the saved were getting revived. The pastor asked me if my schedule would allow us to keep going on. I made a few calls, and we went on for a total of three weeks.

Amid all the blessings of the Lord, it snowed and then iced. But this did not stop the people from coming out to this Holy Ghost filled revival! There is one song that we nearly wore out during this time, "Walk around me Jesus".

Bishop Robert Davis once told me if a farmer goes out to feed his livestock, his cows, and beats the bucket, those cows come running. The farmer dumps bales of hay out for them.

But, if he beats the bucket everyday for a week and the cows come running and he doesn't throw anything out for them to eat, after awhile he beats the bucket and the cows won't budge. They may lift their heads and look, but they are not going to run. Why? Because there isn't any food awaiting them.

People were coming out in bad weather because the Lord, not me, was feeding them. There were several nights I didn't even preach because the power of God was so strong!

So, I always ask the Lord, "As they are beating the bucket in advertising for this revival, give me something to feed them!" I never want anyone to go away *hungry on my part*. There is a great responsibility to being a minister.

"And I will give you pastors according to mine heart, which shall *feed you* with knowledge and understanding". Jer 3:15

I have sat under the ministry of a lot of great pastors who took the time to mentor me. And for that I am appreciative. The Davis's were not only my best friends, but he was a great pastor to me and my family, and Maryann was the best pastor's wife.

It is absolutely wonderful to go to church when you can't wait to hear what your pastor has been preparing for the flock all week. And that is the way it was wherever the Davis's pastored. It's no wonder why God decided to place them in as Overseer in several states now. After all, they really do have the heart of a shepherd.

> 11 And he gave some, *apostles*; and some, *prophets*; and some, *evangelists*; and some, *pastors* and *teachers*; 12 For the perfecting of the saints, for the work of the ministry, for the edifying of the body of Christ: Eph. 4:11-12

March of 1991

I drove to New York for a month of revivals. The first night I spent at the Overseers home. Brother and Sister Trogdon greeted me with arms wide open.

The next day we drove to New York City to a shelter for the homeless. Now, *homeless* is the key word in this story. We were all in this building eating at tables, like a lunch cafeteria.

They had me to bring my guitar and sing to them. Brother Trogdon suggested that I go around and speak to the homeless as they ate their meal.

Well, right off the bat I stuck my foot in my mouth. I was conversing with a table of four when I asked, "So, do y'all live around here?" Did that just come out of my mouth? Really?

I expected them to say, "Yes ma'am. I live under that bridge, and my brother lives in that cardboard box over there". But instead they were very nice. They shook their head in the affirmative direction, smiling the whole time. They could see I was embarrassed and had mercy on me.

I had the best time of my life while I was in New York! The revivals were great and the people were wonderful. The congregations were mostly Jamaicans and knew how to worship the Lord.

I stayed in their homes and ate some of the most wonderful home cooking. There was only one dish I could not eat, the head of the fish. Sister Beulah told me it was the best part.

"You suck the juice out of the head" she said. I told her she could suck the juice out of my fishes head. She laughed and said, "No, you suck your own head!" Other than the head, the rest of the fish was wonderful.

The revivals ran from Sunday morning through Friday night. I had Saturdays off. My Jamaican friend, Rose, was my personal tour guide. We laughed most of the way through the city.

We were standing in line with hopes to be a part of the Phil Donahue audience. We didn't have any tickets, but they told us sometimes the ticket holders didn't show up. So, we were standing in the *non-ticket holders'* line.

All of a sudden, this lady in the ticket holder line walked over to our line. She began walking from the front of the line towards the back. We were in the middle.

When she came to me, she stopped and asked, "Do you have a ticket for the show?" I told her no. She said, "You can have mine as I'm not going today."

I got real excited until I remembered Rose. I replied, "No thank you, I have my friend with me and we need two tickets."

"That's fine" she replied. "I have two tickets. My friend didn't show up and I'm going home." Wow! What are the chances of that? We thanked her and moved over to the ticket holders' line.

The doors opened and we were ushered in. they sat us right down on the very first row! I told Rose, "My mom should be able to see me here!" I had called mom and told her we were going to be on the show, and to look for me in the audience. She was going to set her VCR and record it.

We wanted to know what the show was going to be about, but they wouldn't tell us because they didn't want any preconceived ideas.

They began the count down, 10, 9, 8, 7, 6, 5, 4, "Today's show is going to be about SEX ADDICTION!" What?? "Did he say, sex addiction Rose?" Rose nodded her head yes.

My jaw was in the open position as I could not believe this! "My mom is going to be watching this!" I told Rose, who had her jaw dropped as well. Oh Lord, Oh Lord! What have I got us into?!

The curtain opened and there sat four adults dressed incognito. They looked like undercover agents with their big sunglasses and wigs on. It was the longest hour of my life.

The one lady said she would go to church to pick up men. She said by the time she left, she had a phone number. What? She went to church to pick up men? I'd been going to church for years and hadn't picked one up yet!

Continuing to listen to their stories of being addicted to sex, I saw just how cunning the devil is. Just like all sin, it started out small and grew out of control.

All kinds of advice were given to them, but they seemed to have tried them all without success. I listened intently and realized they were caught in Satan's trap.

At the end of the show, Phil always opened it up to the audience to ask questions. Question after question was hurled at them without a reasonable response.

Phil said, "We have hundreds in this audience, and everyone wants to ask a question!" Then it happened. He ran straight over to me and put the microphone in my hand, and I stood up.

I addressed my question to the lady who had gone to church. "You say you went to church. Did you ever think about talking to the pastor for council? And do you believe in the power of prayer?"

I gave the microphone back to Phil. Phil said, "That's a great question! What do you say?" The lady responded, "I felt too dirty to talk to a pastor, or God."

There you go, I thought! The devil gets you into a situation by telling you it's alright, and then makes you feel too dirty to talk to God about it. Man, he is slick!

There was only one more question after that and the show was over. I walked up onto the stage where they were sitting. I took the lady by the hand and said, "When you die, and one day you will, the only thing that will matter is if you know Jesus as your Savior. He really loves you!"

Tears began to flow from under her dark sunglasses as she squeezed my hand and said, "Thank you." I turned to walk away and walked right into the arms of a security guard! He told me that I was not allowed on the stage. I told him that that was not a problem. In my heart I was saying, "I already did what God wanted me to do."

On our way home, I got to thinking about how God orchestrated the entire event. That lady could have given those two tickets to anyone, but she gave them to us.

We were placed on the very front row, right in front of that lady. Out of hundreds of people, Phil ran over to me. The security guard was kept at bay until I had delivered the message God had sent to that lady.

Isn't God good to us? He cares so much for that lady that He would send a redhead all the way from Arkansas to NYC, just to tell her that He loves her. Now that's love!

During that month I was able to see the Statue of Liberty, the World Trade Center, Twin Towers and so much more. And all on Saturday's. I talked eight friends into going to Madison Square Garden to see the Ringling Brothers Circus. That was fun.

But the very best part of this month in New York were the services! Seeing souls in the altars, crying out to God. I began my last revival at the Bronx on a Sunday morning with over five-hundred in attendance. Everywhere I went, they were all so kind and hospitable to me. New York, I love you!

Reports from Covington Revival March 2009:

Brother Charles Russell and his wife Pastor in Covington, Virginia. I have held a revival there every year since 2005. We have had some great services there, but this one particular revival stands out in my mind. Here are some of the reports from the people themselves, in their own words.

"I had a rare blood disorder and the Lord healed me of it."

"I was healed of chest pain and shortness of breath."

"God healed my knees."

"God healed my hands and blessed my soul."

"God healed me of VERY high Blood Pressure! He has also given me new courage and enthusiasm!"

"God gave me peace to know that everything is going to be alright."

"God healed my tonsils!"

"God healed me of a severe sinus infection. I serve a mighty God!"

"God blessed and healed me."

Two others verbally told me their testimony. God healed me of neuropathy (a painful disease in her feet). The other lady told me that God healed her heart. Isn't God so wonderful?

This is what they wrote in their State Paper:

The revival started off with a great expectation of what God was going to do. We were not disappointed as He showed up in a mighty way! Sunday night God sent His healing waters, and there were so many healed.

Those who walked in with canes, walked out without them! There were many who were dancing in the Spirit. Some looked as though they were doing the Holy Ghost Jitter Bug!!!

A young man walked up to sister Osban with tears running down his face and said, "Sister Kay, I have never been saved and I want to be." Pastor Russell came and we prayed for him and yes, God saved him right then and there!

Attendance was outstanding with an average of 70. Iron Gate blessed us with their singing. Tuesday night the Huddleston church showed up in their nice new bus with 24!

The revival brought Salvation, Healing, and Laughter. After all, laughter does good like a medicine.

Lois

I was in revival in Florida in 2004. It was Sunday morning as I noticed a lady who looked very sad. Her name was Lois Haddad. Her friend, Barbara Lyle, had invited her to the revival.

I did not know what was going on in her life, I just knew by the look on her face that it had to be bad. After the message, I went back to her seat and began to talk with her.

Like so many today, Lois was going through a bad divorce. The Lord told me to tell her something, and I did. "Lois, I know you cannot see this right now, but the sun is going to shine in your life once again."

Lois had grown up attending the Church of God of Prophecy, but had strayed away for several years. But that morning Lois gave her heart back to the Lord.

I flew back to Arkansas, and never heard from her again until the next year in revival. She was still going on with the Lord and her new life.

I never dreamed that out of that revival would come a wonderful friendship. Lois is a lot of fun to be with. She can sure make you laugh! Lois was there during one of the toughest times of my life, when daddy died.

She has become more than a friend, she has become like family. Margie, Quinton, Lois and I always go on vacations together. Quinton doesn't think it's a vacation unless Ms. Lois is along. She can make that boy laugh.

You just might see Lois at one of my revivals helping with the sell of my singing CD's, and now this book! LOL She loves the Lord with all of her heart, and she loves her two grandchildren too. If you are around her for a few minutes, you *will* see pictures of them. And they are beautiful!

It's been nearly ten years now since that revival. It fills my heart with joy to see the ones that you help receive salvation, still continuing on with the Lord.

Testimonies To and From Estes Park, Colorado Retreat

I had to get up at 3:30 to leave at 4:30 to get to Little Rock at 5:30. All I wanted to do was sleep the whole flight. I sat by the window, leaned on my pillow and was ready for a long nap.

A lady sat by me and said, "I don't understand why they split me and my husband up. He is sitting over there." I told her I would be more than willing to change seats with him so they could sit together. She was elated. So, I changed seats with him.

About that time, a young man, Scott, gets on the plane and sat by me. Once again, I leaned back on my pillow ready for sleep. He interrupts me before I can even get to sleep.

He began with, "The last two days have been the pits!"

"Sit up Kay, this man needs to talk" the Lord said.

So, I replied, "I'm sorry". He proceeded to tell me that he was just trying to get back home to see his little girl's recital at school. He said his flight was delayed from Springfield. He then had to rent a car, and spent the night in Branson, Missouri.

The next day he was heading for Little Rock, and a deer ran out and hit the rental car in the driver's door. His door wouldn't open. So every time he needed to get in or out, he had to use the passenger's door.

He got a hotel in Little Rock. The next morning the car battery was dead. He was worried that he would miss his flight (and he nearly did as he was the last one on the plane). But a nice gentleman helped jump his car and get it started. He concluded with, "The last two days have been the pits!"

I said, "I agree with you, your last two days have been a nightmare. But, as bad as it was, I see how God had His hands in it. The deer could have hit in front and come through the windshield and killed you.

He sent a man to help start your car, and He cleared the highway traffic so you could make the flight on time. "

For the next two hours Scott and I talked about how very good God is. By the time the plane had landed, his countenance had gone from gloom and despair to a glowing smiling face. As we touched down, he says, "Do you know what I think? I think God put me right here in this seat next to you today!"

I smiled as the Lord reminded me of the lady who wanted her husband to sit beside her. I made the right move.

Van Ride from Estes Park:

Exhausted from the retreat, I just wanted to rest on the two hour drive to the airport. Sitting on a fifteen passenger van, I snuggled my head on the window.

A fifty-year-old lady sat beside me. She was not a part of the retreat, she was just on her way to the Denver airport. She seemed harmless enough.

Then she said, "My life has really been tough this past six months. I am going through a divorce and I can't seem to cope. I have a lot of fear."

"Sit up Kay, she needs to talk" the Lord said. I sat up.

I replied, "I am so sorry." She began to tell me how she had married late in life, and now he wanted a divorce. She said she had always been self-sufficient, taking care of her own business.

Over the past few years, she had grown to depend on him solely. Now fear had entered her life and she just didn't know what she was going to do? She was a Christian and did not like feeling all of this fear.

I quoted her the verse, "For God hath not given us the spirit of fear; but of power, and of love, and of a sound mind."

"Say that again!" So, I said it again.

"Where is that located in the Bible?" she asked.

"2 Tim 1:7" I said. Now I wish I had brought my Bible on board with me instead of leaving it in my briefcase, which was now packed on the roof of the van. But! I wasn't expecting to minister, I was expecting to sleep.

The entire two hours we conversed back and forth. She practically told me her whole life's story. I encouraged her with scriptures from the Word. This is another good reason to hide the Word of God in our hearts, when your Bible is hidden on the roof of the van!

Anyway, when we arrived at the Denver Airport, as she was going one direction and I was going another, she turned back and said, "Kay, do you know what I think?"

I assured her I did not. She said, "I think God placed us together on this ride. Thanks!" I have often thought about her and how she is doing. One thing I am sure of, she has memorized 2 Timothy 1:7!

Liz in Houston

My flight landed in Houston, Texas. It's funny how they fly you all around the world to get you to Arkansas?

I was waiting for my flight when they announced they had overbooked. I was one of several who were left behind.

We were to spend the night at the Hilton and catch a flight the next morning.

As I was seated on the shuttle that would take me to the Hilton, a young lady, Liz, asked if she could sit by me. I told her sure.

On the short ride there, she told me she was from a small town in Wisconsin and was a little worried about being in this big city. After all, Houston is not a safe place for a single lady to wander around in.

The airline had given us vouchers to eat supper and breakfast at the Hilton. So I told her, "If you would like, I'll meet you at 6:00 and we can dine together." She was happy about that.

During dinner, I told Liz I was a minister. This opened up a door for her. She said she had been raised Catholic, but she was hungry for something more.

Her parents didn't know it, but while at college, Liz had been attending a different church. It was a small Bible church that believed in the Holy Ghost. She said her parents would highly disapprove of it.

She wanted to know if I knew anything about the Holy Ghost. I said, "Yes, in fact I am filled with the Holy Ghost."

"Really?!" she asked with much excitement. Then she floored me when she said, "Speak in tongues!" I laughed and told her it just didn't work like that.

It thrilled me to see someone so *hungry* for more of God! But since she had been raised Catholic, she was so afraid of what her parents might think.

I told her that my friend, Maryann Davis, had been raised Catholic and she is now filled with the Holy Ghost. That seemed to make a difference to her, in a good way.

The steak was really good, but that conversation with Liz was even better. We talked for the longest time before going back to our separate rooms. She seemed more sure about herself.

As she was unlocking her door, she looked back and said, "Miss Kay, I think the Lord put us together this evening." I responded, "Really? I think so too Liz!"

Houston Flight

The next morning I boarded the plane headed to Little Rock. I had been reading the book, "God Catchers". The flight attendant came down the aisle passing out peanuts and drinks.

She asked me what book I was reading. I told her I had already read "God Chasers," and now I was reading "God Catchers." She seemed very interested. Since the book had come with a bookmarker, I gave it to her so she could remember the name.

"I'll be back as soon as I finish serving everyone", she said. I was sitting on the outside aisle seat. When she came back, she knelt down beside me and said, "Life has been so hectic the past two days and I've been asking God why?"

I responded, "Maybe God is stretching you." When I said that, she began to cry. I thought, then again, maybe not! Lol

She continued to tell me what was going on in her life that had her so distraught. As God gave me words to say, I would tell them to her. Soon the flight was over.

As we were all making our exit out of the plane, the attendants were standing there thanking us for flying with them. When it was my turn to go, she pulls me aside and asked if I would wait a minute. I told her sure.

She wasn't finished talking yet. So after awhile, we said our goodbyes. She asked me, "If you are ever in the Houston area, would you consider going to church with me? If you met my pastor, maybe he would have you come and conduct us a revival."

I told her I would be glad to. We exchanged phone numbers and I was on my way. After all, Wilma was waiting for me in baggage.

I felt like the Lord had me minister more on the way to and from the retreat, than He did at the retreat! Isn't it just like God to place all of us intentionally, in places He needs us to minister for Him?

My Prayers

Everyday I have several prayers I pray. I begin with the Lord's Prayer. I thank Him for all He has, and is doing for me. I begin it with praise and end with praise. I like what I heard someone once say, "Life is a gift, prayer is a thank you note!"

Then I pray what is known as the Jabez Prayer. I switch it up to fit me. "I ask You to bless me indeed today. Bless my family, church, friends, finances and my health. Extend my territory according to Your purpose and will. Let Your hand and anointing go with me, and chase evil far from me. Please don't let me hurt anyone."

Then I begin to plead the blood of Jesus over a multitude of family and friends. I ask God to bless Israel and to give their leader wisdom, knowledge and understanding. I pray for the President of the United States to do right in the eyes of God.

I then speak blessings over *everyone* who is blessing me and over the churches I have come out of revival that month. There are two churches who give monthly into my ministry, I call them out by name and ask God to bless them.

When I am finished, I ask for wisdom, knowledge and understanding for myself, some Pastors, my State Overseer and few more Overseer's, the General Overseer, and the Presbyter for North America.

Then I pray for those who have requested prayer from me. Whether it be Spiritual, financial, physical or whatever it might be. Then I end in thanking God for allowing me to minister for Him.

This always seems to get the day going in the right direction. I feel like prayer is an honor and a privilege. God made a way for all mankind to communicate with Him.

Prayer should never become a *"Santa List"* of all the things we want, and what can you do for me God. There are times that I just bust out with a *"I love You God!"* while driving down the road. Have a life of praise and thanksgiving.

Here is something that is good to do at least once a year; read six chapters from the book of Psalms and one chapter from the book of Proverbs. In thirty days, one month, you will have completely read both books. Psalms teaches you how to praise, and Proverbs teaches you how to live.

You Have the Right to Remain Silent

When I read this article from my friend, Stephanie Thompson, I knew I needed to include it in this book. It kind of gives us a check up, from the neck up! Thanks Stephanie for these great words of wisdom.

> You have the right to remain silent. We all have heard these words. The Miranda Warning... You have the right to remain silent. Anything you say can and will be used against you in a court of law. You have the right to speak to an attorney, and to have an attorney present during any questioning. If you cannot afford a lawyer, one will be provided for you at government expense.
>
> We know that these are quoted to those who are being questioned or arrested by the police. However, have you ever thought of these words and considered applying them to your own life?

There are times in life when we should remain silent. Over the past four years, God has taken me on a journey of silence. Not a vow of silence but a journey. Anyone who knows me understands that I generally have an opinion and am very vocal so the act of silence is definitely a God-act. I've learned many valuable lessons while being silent.

I've seen into the hearts of many; the good and the bad. I've been taught so much about myself that I could not have learned if not silent. I've found that you can hear much better the thoughts and intents of others and most importantly the Voice of God while being silent.

I've learned that so many times in so many situations silence is the preferred response. When Jesus faced the Sanhedrin in Matthew 26:63... He remained silent.

In Matthew 27:12 when Jesus faced Pilate and the chief priests accused him.... He (Jesus) remained silent. In Psalm 4:4, David tells us, don't sin by letting anger control you. Think about it overnight and remain silent.

Recently when I was going through a stressful time of being falsely accused and slandered, God gave me the scriptures in Exodus 14:13-14 (MSG) Moses spoke to the people:

"Don't be afraid. Stand firm and watch GOD do his work of salvation for you today. Take a good look at the Egyptians today for you're never going to see them again. GOD will fight the battle for you. And you? You keep your mouths shut!"

God, through His Word spoke to me to not say a word, to hold my peace and let Him deal with those who set out to destroy me. He gave me the right to remain silent.

I've found during my journey that remaining silent is not easy but most definitely necessary. The beginning of my silence lesson started about four years ago.

I sat silent as I watched adults talk about one of my boys. I sat silent as I watched him struggle through this time knowing he had done no wrong but was treated as though he had anyway.

I watched in silence as he was treated unjustly never bringing out that fact to those who caused this pain. It was one of the hardest things I've ever done.

On several occasions during this time, I would sit in this group of peers hiding behind my sunglasses as tears ran down my face knowing my child didn't deserve this but knowing a bigger lesson was being taught. It was as if my heart was ripped out, and possibly was.

I discovered however that those mangled portions were being replaced with something better. During this time, I learned patience, self-control, kindness, and long suffering; those fruits of the Spirit that we sometimes have so much trouble with.

Self-control kept me from speaking; for it would have done more harm than good. Patience and long-suffering kept me continuing down this path to which there was no foreseeable end. It kept me silent in my chair when I sincerely wanted no part of silence.

Kindness kept me from treating them as my flesh wanted to. To act like a momma bear protecting her cubs. But what good would that have done? I would have ostracized us. I would have been seen as out of control, and I would have lost any Christian witness that I might have. So, I sat in silence.

Sitting in silence did not tell my son that I didn't care or love him. It didn't tell him that I wouldn't stand up for him, but it taught him that sometimes in life it's not about being right or treated fairly but sometimes there is a bigger picture, a larger lesson, and a deeper learning that is necessary to make us who God desires us to be.

I've watched in admiration of him as just this last week, he was telling me a story of something that had happened, and I asked "well, did you say so and so?". He said, "no, mom, that would have done no good and perhaps caused problems." I think perhaps he got it. He too has learned... we do have the right to remain silent.

Just as the Miranda Warning tells us that "anything you say can and will be held against you", we can rest assured that those words are true. Matthew 12:36 says, "But I say to you that for every idle word men may speak, they will give account of it in the day of judgment." When we read that we think... really? I'm here to say... really! Idle words are negative and useless words that produce no good effect. Words that harm.

I've been guilty of using idle words. I'll be the first to admit that; however through this journey of silence I've learned that those idle words become less and less spoken because of the consciousness of the great impact of words.

I've discovered in remaining silent that we can keep others from being hurt, offended, and sinning. Matthew 18:6 says "Whoever causes one of these little ones who believe in Me to sin, it would be better for him if a millstone were hung around his neck, and he were drowned in the depth of the sea."

Wow, it would be better to have a huge weight tied around your neck and thrown into the ocean and drown than to cause someone else to sin. Can our words do that? Yes! When we talk about our offenses to another person, we are causing that person to think negatively about someone else.

When we "share" our latest story of what another said to us that hurt our feelings, we are not speaking what is "good, what edifies or imparts grace" (Ephesians 4:29) We are speaking words that could cause someone to feel uncomfortable around another.

Our words could cause them to take sides in a situation that has nothing whatsoever to do with them. Our words can even cause them to sin by being angry or becoming bitter toward another.

Causing another Christian to sin is in and of itself sin; therefore, we should be very cautious when we speak. We should be aware of how our words and actions may affect others. We have the right to remain silent.

During my journey of silence, I've had situations arise that absolutely no one knows about because I've chosen to only tell God... not even my husband. Now you may be thinking that I'm wrong for "keeping secrets" from my spouse, but I can whole-heartedly tell you that I am not. I've heard God's voice telling me to remain silent. If I had told him certain happenings, he would feel differently toward certain people and he may not be comfortable around them and I may cause him to sin by my words.

Proverbs 11: 13 says, "A talebearer reveals secrets, but he who is of a faithful spirit conceals a matter."

I'm here to tell you that everyone in your home, family, church, or circle of friends does not need to know every negative, hurtful, or offense that happens to you. They can't do anything about it anyway, and we shouldn't risk causing someone else to sin because we couldn't get over the fact that something negative happened to me.

We just need to suck it up, know that life sometimes hurts, and learn to rely on God to deal with situations and problems. We need to not cause others to fall because we can't remain silent. We have the right to remain silent.

God has shown me so much during this journey of silence. I still am opinionated but I've learned (most of the time) to wait on someone to ask my opinion. I have learned that words are not necessary. I've learned that it's best when giving an answer to use Scripture.... which is the Voice of Truth.

I've learned to limit my exposure to those who use too many words for they are many times negative, gossips, and hurtful to others. I've learned that Proverbs 10:19 is true, "In the multitude of words sin is not lacking but he who restrains his lips is wise." I've learned that God can fix problems much better than I can.

I've learned that speaking up for myself, or those I love is not necessary. For God is our Protector and Defender! I've learned that, "Whoever guards his mouth and tongue keeps his soul from troubles" (Proverbs 21:23).

I've learned that "a word fitly spoken is like apples of gold in settings of silver" (Proverbs 25:11). I've learned that, "A fool vents all his feelings, but a wise man holds them back" (Proverbs 29:11).

I've learned that the funny quote is true... Silence is golden but duct tape is silver and that sometimes we need duct tape because we fail miserably at the silence part!

I'm sure I will continue on my journey of silence for a while longer. James 3:8 says "But no man can tame the tongue", but I'm here to tell you that God certainly can and He has. I think the most important thing is that I've learned that... I have the right to remain silent.
©Stephanie Thompson July 21, 2011

Chapter 9
DIARY OF A BROKEN ANKLE

March 16, 2003
"Rejoice not against me, O mine enemy: for **when I fall, I shall arise**..." Micah 7:8

Monday night, March 10th 2003 at 9:30 I was at my Cousin Joe's welding shop in Harrisburg, Arkansas. I fell and broke two bones in my left ankle, crushed other bones in it and dislocated the leg bone from the foot bone.

As I raised myself up to a sitting position, I looked down at my foot and noticed it was turned around the wrong direction. Instead of looking at my toes, I was looking at my heel.

"Don't touch me," I told Joe as I reached into my coat pocket for my cell phone, "my foot is broken."

I dialed 911 and immediately remembered I had *no* medical insurance. I hit end and called my dad. "Dad, my ankle is broken and I need you to take me to the hospital. I'm at Joe's shop."

I asked Joe to move the pick up truck and bring my purse to me. I called Margie and told her what had happened and asked her to pray and to call around for prayer. I also called Linda Beal and asked for prayer from Oklahoma.

Dad arrived and he and Joe picked me up and carried me to the car. On the way I said, "Dad-gum-it dad! We were supposed to go fishing tomorrow!" His response was, "It won't keep me from going." That's dad!

On the 20-mile ride to the Jonesboro hospital, dad couldn't find the flashers. I was holding my ankle in my lap, and reached up and pressed the flasher button. Dad was shook up somewhat, so I helped him click his seatbelt.

He was driving 80 miles an hour as we passed a police car sitting on the side of the road.

He put his lights on and began in hot pursuit. Dad paid no attention to him. Finally I said, "I think you might need to pull over." Against his will, he did.

I was in a lot of pain, and as he came to the window, dad said, "My daughters' foot is broken and I am taking her to the hospital." The officer shined his light on the deformed looking ankle I held in my hands and said, with a painful look on his face, "Drive careful."

When we arrived at the hospitals E. R., they began to work on me. The nurse on duty, Sandy, was very kind. She said she was going to have to cut my jeans off. I begged her not to, telling her they were new. She assured me they would have to.

She went to my sock with her scissors and I said, "Please don't cut my sock!" She said that I could try to take it off myself, if I wanted to. After trying for 10 seconds I decided, "Oh well, socks aren't that expensive!" She cut it off.

I still insisted that my jeans (they were new!) could be saved. I pulled the right leg out and they were able to thread the jeans over my left leg and broken ankle. I was thankful.

I kept telling them that I had NO insurance at all and that I could not spend the night. The nurse informed me that I would be spending several nights.

The pain became more severe by the minute. They began to get an I. V. started and shot of pain medication into me.

Much to everyone's amazement, the powerful shots were not taking effect at all. They continued to give me more. I continued to maintain consciousness and make calls for prayer on my cell phone. By 12:30 a.m. I was in a world of hurt. I continued to hold conversations with my dad, aunt, three cousins and a pastor.

Dad told the nurse, "If you want her out, you'll have to knock her out!"

During this time they did blood work on me and an EKG. The anesthesiologist came and began his work. I have never known pain like this before. I began to go into shock. At 1:00 a.m. they took me to surgery. The anesthesiologist put me out and the doctor began.

To their surprise, in the middle of the surgery I sat straight up on the operating table. All I can remember seeing are the doctors eyes bugged out at me through his mask with his beanie hat on. The nurses said, "Miss Osban, you must lay down!" I replied, "Oh, alright." And I did.

Surgery was over around 4:00 a.m. and I was taken to a hospital room. They had placed a plate with ten screws and pins in my ankle. I awoke at 5:00 a.m. with my relatives in the room with me. I told them I was going to sleep and they needed to go home and do the same.

For the next 24 hours I wouldn't know what world I was in. They had me so drugged with pain medication. I had several calls (at least that is what I am told) that I would never remember, not even to this day. One of them was Ron, a member of the church where I pastored. He said, "How are you Sister Kay?" I said, "Who are you?" Ron said, "It's me, Ron." I told him that I did not know a Ron and that my room number was 217 and that I was going to hang up, and I did.

I had called another member and left a message on their answering machine. They say it was hilarious to listen to. My words were slurred and I gave the wrong phone number and wrong room number.

I even called my aunt Diane and told her I had fallen out of the back of a truck and broke my ankle. Everyone has their own stories about their conversations with me. I even told another member, Leslie, not to come to the hospital because the price of gas was too high.

Around 5:00 a.m. Wednesday morning, I asked the nurse to let up on the pain medication so I could think straight, and they did.

By 8 a.m. I asked to see the bill so far. They brought the hospital bill of $5,300.00. This did not include the surgery, doctor and all the other specialists. This was just for the one and a half days in the hospital and the medication they gave me.

I told them that they were too high and that the Holiday Inn was a bit cheaper, and I would be checking out. The doctor came in and advised against it, as he wanted me there a few more days because of the severity of the injury. Once again I told them that I had no insurance and that I would be leaving.

My dad came at noon and took me to his house. I spent the night with him and Ruth. They waited on me hand and foot.

The next day Wilma and Charlie Gentle (my Godparents) came and took me to their home in Gurdon (40 miles from my house). I was weak from the trip and spent the night with them.

They also took very good care of me. They brought me home Friday at 5:00 p.m. where I was met by my neighbor, Mr. Peevy. He helped unload my stuff.

Margie and Quinton got to the house at 6 and began taking care of me. They spent the night with me and took very good care of me, doing laundry and cooking. Quinton was only 6, but he was a great help to his aunt Kay-Kay.

I had to walk with a walker, I could not put any weight on my left foot that was in a cast. So I hopped with a walker. Every time I needed to go to the bathroom, Quinton would walk beside me and hold his arms out. He said, "Kay-Kay, if you fall, I will catch you." He is so very sweet!

Some of my members came to visit, and put up a handrail outside. I attended church the next morning, but I had someone else deliver the message.

The doctors said it would be a very long road to recovery.

Saturday March 29, 2003
Hello Everyone!

It's me again. I have been getting a lot of e-mail asking how I am doing. So, here is the info.

I left Hope Monday afternoon, headed to Jonesboro to spend the night with the Vickers, because my doctor appointment was Tuesday morning at 8:30. Before I left, I stopped at the post office to get stamps and my mail.

I was by myself as I climbed the steps with my crutches. It was 80 degrees and pretty. I felt so good being able to climb all those steps, all except the last one.

That is when my crutch got caught on the last step and I fell forward, spreading myself all over the concrete. I hit my knee, the knee on my bad foot. One crutch flew one way and the other flew the other way. I could not get up.

A kind man ran over, kneeling beside me and asked me, "Oh my, are you hurt?" I looked up at him and said, "Just my pride, please help me up." About that time, a kind lady gathered my crutches up and brought them to me. They were able to get me up as I assured them I was alright.

My knee was all skinned up and killing me, BUT, I was alright. One of my crutches had lost the bottom rubber tip off, so the man brought it to me. As he was putting it back on, he said, "Looks like you threw a shoe." We had a good laugh. I got in line to buy stamps and he was behind me (probably making sure I wouldn't fall again!)

After I bought stamps, I turned to him to thank him once again. He said, "If you will wait for me, I will help you down those steps." I assured him I would wait.

He carried my mail to the car, and there it was, a red wasp (I am allergic to them) flying around my head. It landed on my door handle. I asked him to kill it with my mail and he did. He laughed and said, "Now wouldn't that have been the icing on the cake, after you took the fall, then to be stung by a wasp!"

I Still Say God is Good, all the Time!!

I was concerned that I might have done some damage to my already injured ankle. But when I got to the doctor's office the next morning, he said I was healing up really great.

I told him, "What can you expect; I have a good doctor and **Jesus**!" He agreed. He saw the bruise and skinned up knee and looked at me with raised eyebrows, I said, "I was really doing good until yesterday when I fell and went boom." But there was *no* extra damage to my ankle due to the fall. Thank the Lord!

I looked at my ankle and saw the 5 to 6 inch incision on the outside and the 3 inch incision on the inside. It was held together with lots of staples. They pulled all the staples out (not pleasant) and put a cast on. I wanted a *green* one, but they were out, so I chose a beautiful "purple" cast.

He asked me if I wanted a $250.00 walking boot or a $75.00 walking shoe for the cast, I took the shoe. He is a very good doctor. I will get this cut off April the 23rd. He told me he put 10 screws, a plate and many pins in my ankle.

I left there and went to the hospital to have them go over my bill for me. I just thought that $5,000 was high, that is until I received the final bill from the hospital of $16,500! As they were explaining the bill to me, I found out they charged me $1,600.00 for 8 screws. I thought $200.00 a screw was a bit high until I saw that the other two screws were $2,200.00. "That's $1,100.00 per screw!" I said to the lady across the desk from me, "Don't you think that is a little bit too high for two screws?" She replied, "What did you want us to do, go to the local hardware store and get some?" I said, "Sounds like a plan to me."

Anyway, I was able to get them to knock some off from the bill. This is what they knocked off, a three-dollar box of Kleenex that I did not even get!

I want to thank all of you who have prayed for me because I know it is the Lord who is doing the work. My ankle is healing very well. I thank all the churches and individuals who have sent love offerings to help with the medical expenses.

The cards have been uplifting and I have had many good laughs over a lot of them. Two doctors in Oklahoma have treated me at no expense to me, you know who you are. You **all** have been so very kind. There are no words to express my gratitude for all your prayers and everything you've done.

Love to all,

Kay (Also known as *Hop-a-long*, *Chester* and *Skippy*!)

Compassion of a Child

My ankle was still in the healing process. I went to Wal-Mart, got in the electric wheelchair/shopping cart.

While going down an aisle, a little boy (probably three years old) saw me. He broke loose from his mothers hand and ran to me. Putting his hand on my cast, he looked into my eyes and asked, "Does it hurt?"

"No honey, not really".

By this time his mother was running toward her son. She took his hand and apologized to me. I assured her an apology was not necessary, that he was not bothering me in the least bit.

As they walked away, he turned back at me and gave me the biggest smile. Smiles like that are better than any medicine the world has to offer! Children, I love them!

CHAPTER 10
IT COULD ONLY HAPPEN TO ME

The Attack of Ceiling Fans

In 1985 Margie had moved into a double wide trailer in Hoopa, California. I was there visiting mom and dad during Christmas vacation. Margie needed a ceiling fan put in her dining room. At this time, I had never installed a ceiling fan. But I volunteered to do it. I knew that between Margie and I, we could get the job done. And with mom as the supervisor, this was a done deal!

Mom thought it would be a great idea to video record the process. When I got the light fixture down, and there was nothing but bare wires hanging down, mom turned the video camera on. It was lights, camera, and action! When Margie and I got the housing unit installed, mom was really excited to show that on film. Then we got the fan blades on.

Margie and I were using her kitchen table as a ladder. We completed installing the last fan blade. It was finished. Now if it would work.

Mom said, "Wait until I turn on the video camera before you pull the chain to see if it works." I looked at Margie and she had her head between blades. I had a thought. It was a mischievous thought. My thinking was, if I turn this on, and I duck my head, the fan blade will hit Margie in the nose. Ready, set, go!

I pulled the chain. Now to my great surprise, the motor was in reverse. Before I could duck, the blade whacked me on the forehead! Boy howdy, I saw stars!

For some unknown reason, mom thought this was hilarious! She was laughing so hard that the camera was shaking. Margie was faster at ducking than I was, and not one blade touched a hair on her head!

Meanwhile, I was holding my forehead and looking for blood. While holding my head, I politely asked mom to turn off the camera. But there was no way she was going to do that. She knew a good show when she saw one.

Again I asked her, with a little more authority in my voice, to turn the camera off. Nope, she wasn't going to do it. Only until she and Margie had had a good laugh did she do so. That video was nearly worn out in the spot that they rewound over and over and over again! The good news is that the fan worked great, and I lived to tell about it.

Fast forward to 2005

20 years later Margie had bought a house across the street from me in Hope, Arkansas. Once again, I was installing a ceiling fan for her. This time it was in her living room.

We were almost killed or maimed. As Margie was getting down (I was still on my ladder) the housing from the fan fell (it was barely hanging on by a screw that let go). Anyway, it hit me on my right wrist, grazed Margie's head, knocked me off the ladder landing me on the ankle that I crushed a year earlier and threw me on the couch! I landed on a knife and a light globe. Margie escaped by out running it. Me, it just bounced all over my body before hitting the floor.

Then when we got it put back together, I got the wires all together, she turned it on and it only wanted to work when she was turning it off. Now I know Margie was thinking, "Kay has broken it!" But, being the electrician I am, (LOL) I knew she had a faulty light switch. So, I went home and got my supply and replaced both the switches to the outside light and the living room.

It works great now, and is one of the prettiest ones I have seen. Praise God once again I lived to tell the story!

Bless Margie's heart; she must dread working with me. I have installed about 50 ceiling fans in my life, but this one really attacked me!

About a Year Later

I was visiting my friends, Norma & Henry Schneider in Broken Arrow, Oklahoma. While they were gone to the store I decided to do something nice for them. Norma had said she was going to clean the top of the kitchen cabinets. Now, I'd say they were about 15 feet high.

So I climbed up a tall ladder. I'd clean a section, move the ladder and repeated this several times. Then it happened. I took a step higher on the ladder and WHAM! I got hit in the back of the head with a ceiling fan going full speed! I saw little birdies flying around in a circle. The two ceiling fans from the past flashed before my eyes. I got down off the ladder, regained my consciousness, and finished the job. I'm not a quitter!

On a Yet Funnier Note

Back in the early 90's I was visiting my good friends Helen Jones and Linda Beal in Duncan, Oklahoma.

Helen had a ceiling fan that Linda liked, and Linda had one that Helen liked. Both fans were attached to ceilings. But I told them that this was not a problem, that I was the *"ceiling fan whisperer"*.

I took down both fans and put Helen's over at Linda's house, and Linda's at Helen's house. Both friends were happy. By the way, they lived across the street from each other. I also would like to add that this all happened without incident!

Later on that evening Helen came over to Linda's. I asked, "How are you enjoying your fan?" She said, "You know what? Every time I turn *my* switch on, Linda's fan comes on across the street!"

It really threw me for a second. I said, "Really?" She couldn't hold a straight face any longer and busted out laughing. I knew I had been had!

Here's Your Sign

Have you ever wondered why certain things are done? For instance, why do they sterilize the needle for lethal injections? I mean, these are just random thoughts that run through my head from time to time.

Then there are those times when I say something that makes sense to me... until they come out of my mouth.

Margie and I were conversing one day about her not sleeping well at night. I told her that each night before I go to bed I take two Benadryl and that really helps me sleep.

She said, "Kay, you might get addicted to them." Now, this is what I am talking about. I opened my mouth and this is what came out... "I will not! I've been taking them for over ten years!" Margie looked at me and raised her eyebrows. It was then that I had a thought... maybe, just maybe I was already addicted!

Here's your sign Kay.

I think it may be Hereditary

But this doesn't just happen to me. One day it happened to Margie. I think it may be hereditary. I asked her to button the back button on my blouse. Margie noticed a red mark at the base of my neck.

She inquired what it was. I told her it was my birthmark (are you ready for this, here it comes). She asked, "Well, how long have you had it?" I then looked at her and raised my eyebrows. She knew she had been had.

Before I could have the pleasure to say, "Well Margie, lets see. I sort of remember getting it at birth, you know, since it's a *BIRTHMARK*!" But she just looked at me and said, "Just shut-up". Here's *your* sign Margie!

Parvo

I have to tell this story. I know my friend; Carl "Doc" Davis in Tulsa, Oklahoma, (who is a Veterinarian) will really get a kick out of this.

Some friends and I were talking one day about dogs. I was young and had no idea that *parvo* was a disease that affected dogs. They were telling me about someone who had several dogs. They began naming them.

I was amazed at the number of dogs! Then they said the guy had Parvo in the backyard. My eyes widened as I exclaimed, "They have another dog and named it Parvo!"

I thought they would never stop laughing! I had no idea what was so funny. They explained what Parvo was. This time I handed myself the sign!

Please, no more pictures!

Back when I first began to evangelize, there was one thing I dreaded, the family photo album! Invariably, the pastor's wife would bring out the photo albums.

I saw hundreds of pictures of people I did not know. Children, grandchildren, brothers, sisters, mothers, fathers, grandparents, aunts, uncles, church members from past and present churches and all the family pets!

When this first began, I thought it was nice. But after a number of years, I'd see her coming with stacks of albums and my heart would sink.

It's quite different nowadays; we all whip out our cell phones and show off our families. At least our cell phones are not nearly as heavy as all those photo albums!

How's the Lemonade?

Cathy Brown, her mother Betty Powell and I were in Texarkana having lunch. I was *between* revivals and was really having to watch my nickels.

We went dutch and all ordered the *special*. They ordered ice tea with their meal. I really wanted ice tea, but knew I couldn't afford it. So I ordered *water with lemon*. They brought me water with lemon. But it wasn't a lemon slice stuck to the top of your glass. It was packets of lemon juice. So I squeezed the lemon juice into the water and added sugar.

Betty and Cathy didn't know I was *"financially embarrassed"* and asked me how that tasted? I said, "Oh, it's really not bad. Besides, they want too much for their tea."

Towards the end of the meal I told them I needed to make a confession. It tasted awful, but the meal was very delicious.

As we were at the register paying out, I said, "Please don't charge me for a drink as I drank water." The lady replied, "The meal included the drink ma'am".

Cathy and Betty wanted to bust out laughing right then and there! Thankfully they waited until we got outside. I can remember it so well, all three of us leaned up against the wall, holding our belly and laughing!

Even though it's been several years ago, if it's via email, Facebook, text, phone call or in person, all one has to do is mention lemonade to get the laughter flowing!

I Know Who You Are!

About 30 years ago, I visited a local church in Arkansas. I was the guest speaker for the night. After church, they paid me in cash.

I headed home and pulled into the first gas station I saw, and I filled up. I think it was $25.00. I went inside and paid with the money I had received that night. All the money was one dollar bills.

So I stood at the counter and counted out 25 one dollar bills. The lady looked at me and smiled and said, "I know who you are!"

All of a sudden, I felt very *special*, she knew me! As she gathered up the one dollar bills, she continued, "You're a waitress!" I just smiled. I was too embarrassed to tell her I was a minister that had just come from a *oneness* church! Lol

I clearly called shotgun, but he put me in the backseat anyway!

One beautiful April weekend Lois and I went to the Virginia Ladies Retreat. My friend Judy Schall was the guest speaker. Sunday morning we headed back to Georgia. I was driving and began to get real sleepy so I asked Lois to drive. I had been asleep for two hours when I heard Lois say, "What's up with that?"

I sat up to learn she had ran us out of gas! It was 90 degree, but we managed to pull under a grove of shade trees. I called 911, they sent out a police car and I agreed to go with him while Lois stayed with the car.

We were five miles from a station. As I went to get into the police car, I pulled on the *FRONT* door handle, it was locked.

The officer informed me I had to ride in the back. OK, since I had *NEVER* been in the back seat of a police car, I had no idea what I was getting myself into.

When the door shut, I felt all the air suck out of that car. My knees were in my chest as there is NO room in the back seat! There was a solid sheet of steel on the back of the front seat, bars on the windows and a small peak-a-boo window that you can see the officer.

I have a real problem being in small, enclosed places and I hate elevators! I thought I would die before we got to the station. I told the officer that I had a real problem, it is called **CLAUSTROPHOBIA**! I said, "As soon as the car stops, will you please hurry and open my backdoor?" He agreed to do so. He was a really nice guy.

I bought a gas can and as he was pumping gas into it, I said, "I am BEGGING (yes! I begged!) you to let me ride in the front seat!" He said with compassion in his voice, "I wish I could, but it is against the law. I could lose my job." I thought about telling him he could always get another job, but decided against it.

I asked him how far the next exit would be before we could turn around to get back to the car. He said he had authority to turn around wherever he wanted. DUH!!!

When we got back onto I-95, he floored it. I looked through the peep hole and saw he was driving 95 MPH. I thought, "I love this man!" My next thought was, "I'd bet you this puppy could go 110! WOW! 95 MPH on I-95! I wish we were on I-295!"

Sure enough, he flipped around and pulled behind my car where Lois was waiting with a big smile. After putting the gas in the car, he said, "I suggest you ladies take the next exit and get some gas." I turned to look at him and saw he was smiling!

As we drove off, I turned to Lois and told her the next time she runs out of gas, SHE would be the one riding in the backseat of a police car!

I told her about the ride. She laughed and told me how scared I looked in the backseat as the cop car flew by. I told her I didn't think it was all that funny. She replied, "Well, I took your picture as you were getting into the cop car and it will be on Facebook tomorrow!"

I looked at her with unbelief as she quickly said, "Just kidding. I wanted to but was afraid the officer would take my camera away from me".

"Spit that out of Your Mouth!"

I was traveling east on I-40, running a little late for a revival in W. Helena when I met a Policeman traveling west. I looked and noticed I was speeding (I know this is a surprise to everyone!) He flipped around and pulled in behind me. As I pulled over, the car in front of me pulled over as well. I thought, "Great, now he has both of us!"

The officer asked to see my driver's license and told me to sit still as he was going to speak to the gentleman in front of me.

I watched as he had a rather long conversation with him, then asked him to step out of his car. As the two of them walked by me, the officer said, "Miss Osban, I will be right back after I take care of him." Well, I was just left there to sit, and so I did.

Meanwhile, I put some gum in my mouth and began to chew it as I watched the happenings in my rearview mirror.

The man was told to stand at the front of the Police car, which also put him at the back of my car. I watched him as he paced back and forth from one end of my bumper to the other.

All of a sudden, the officer yells at him on the bullhorn, "Stand still!" The man stood still. I thought to myself, "That officer must be a pretty tough guy. He won't even let the poor man walk around to stretch his legs." I continued to look and chew my gum.

About that time he yells out over the bullhorn, "**SPIT THAT OUT OF YOUR MOUTH!**" I thought to myself, "Just when is it a crime to sit in your *own* car and chew gum?" But, I was obedient.

I took the gum out of my mouth, but I didn't bend down to put the gum in the trash because I was afraid the officer would think I was reaching for a gun. So, I tossed the gum towards my trash bag down by my leg. After that, I placed both hands upon my steering wheel so he could easily see them.

I sat like that for quite awhile. Finally he put the man in the backseat of the police car and came up to me. He said, "Miss Osban, I know you probably don't understand what just happen." By this time, I didn't care why he wanted me to spit my gum out, I just wanted out of there.

He proceeded to explain, "You see Miss. Osban, the man is drunk and he knew I was going to be giving him a breath analysis test. That is why he put a Cert in his mouth and that is why I ask him to *spit it out*."

It was at that time I wanted to bust out laughing, but instead I said, "I understand officer." I signed my ticket and drove off laughing at myself.

When I told mom, she laughed and laughed and laughed! When she finally quit laughing, and could get her breath, she asked me, "Did you tell the officer that you spit out your gum?" I said, "No! I wasn't going to give him that much joy, especially after he gave me a speeding ticket!"

Where Will You Wake Up?

I was on my way to Georgia from Arkansas. Lois was with me. After driving ten hours, I began to get very sleepy (again!). So I ask Lois if she would drive so I could sleep. She agreed. Now I admit, I am not a good passenger, not at all! As I leaned my seat back, I said, "Please don't kill me." She said, "Lean back and go to sleep. You'll either wake up at home or in Heaven!" Suddenly I wasn't sleepy anymore!

Virginia Hokies

While in revival at Fieldale, Virginia (now Ridgeway) with Pastor Bud Sedwick, I had a sermon *"blooper"*. In the middle of my message it seemed as though everyone got really quiet.

Wanting to get them *"stirred up"* again, I said, "I am an Arkansas Razorback fan. And when I am watching them play, I get very excited!" Then I did the "Woo-Pig-Sooie" call, raising my hands in the air as only a true Razorback fan can do.

Then I said, "I know that you Virginia fans get excited about the *HOOTERS*." They all began to snicker. It was at that moment I realized that I meant to say, "Virginia Hokies" (Virginia's mascot).

Immediately I said, "You did not hear me say Hooters, you heard me say Hokies!" But there was no doubt in their minds what they had heard. BUT! The excitement was back in the congregation again!

I'm an Angel?

Lois and I were on our way back to Georgia, from Virginia. We stopped at the North Carolina rest area.

As I was washing my hands, Lois said, "I hear someone crying for help".

"You do?" I listened and sure enough, I heard it too. An elderly lady was crying out, "Someone, please help me. I have fallen and I can't get up".

I walked down to the handicapped stall and looked under the door. There she was, laying on the floor with blood running down her face.

Since the door was locked, I got on my back and scooted under it and unlocked it. I lifted her up and sat her down on the toilet.

She had a cut above her eye from where she had fallen. A lady saw what was going on and came over to us. She said she was a nurse.

While she and Lois looked after her, I ran to my car and got the first-aid kit and some peroxide. We took her to the Visitors Center where they took down all the facts.

As she was relating it to the attendant, she said, "This lady crawled (I scooted) under the stall and got me up. I tell you, she's an angel, an absolute angel!"

I looked just in time to see Lois rolling her eyes. The lady just kept on about her ordeal. Her husband was very appreciative as well.

I couldn't help it, when we got in the car I looked at Lois and said, "Did you hear that? I'm an angel!" There go those eyes rolling again!

What Shall I Do With This Goat?

In the early 80's I was visiting my granny James in Harrisburg. While there, I decided to go to a livestock auction with my aunt Augustine.

We were sitting midway up top on the bleachers when they brought a goat out. As I sat there, I wondered, who wants a goat? Then I saw my cousin Marlin enter and I frantically waved my hand to let him know where we were sitting.

I just bought a goat! The auctioneer thought I was bidding as he saw my arms flaying around! Aunt Augustine asked me, "So Kay, what are you going to do with a goat?"

I could just see me driving down the road with a goat in my tiny Toyota. I prayed, "Lord, please let someone else bid." About that time a man made another bid.

What a relief! Then the auctioneer began his jibber and was looking my way. By this time I was sitting on my hands. He kept looking at me to bid. I just shook my head "no" and the other man was the proud owner of a black and white goat!

Aunt Betty

Some years ago my aunt Betty was having knee surgery at Fort Smith, Arkansas. I was not in revival that week and told her I would come and be with her.

They had her all prepped for surgery, so I went back to have prayer for her. I think she was behind sheet number three. I peeked my head in, and there she lay.

The nurse had put a black X on the knee that needed surgery. When the nurse left I told Aunt Betty, "It's a good thing she did that. You wouldn't want the wrong knee operated on!"

Then I felt like being a little mischievous, I know, it's hard to believe isn't it! I asked her if she had read the Arkansas Gazette last week. She had not.

I proceeded to tell her about a lady who was diabetic and had to have her right leg cut off. But the doctor made a mistake and cut off her left leg instead. Then he had to cut off her other leg.

Aunt Betty was appalled! "If I were her, I'd sue that doctor!" she said. I told Aunt Betty that she couldn't sue because..."she didn't have a leg to stand on!"

She said, "You crazy thing! Here I am about to have my knee operated on and you tell me that!"

We were laughing when the nurse walked in and said it was time to take her away.

I asked the nurse if I could have a moment to pray with my aunt, to which she gladly agreed. I kissed Aunt Betty on the forehead and told her I would be here when she came to.

As I was walking towards the waiting room, I overheard my aunt ask the nurse, "Did you happen to read the Arkansas Gazette last week... "And I laughed!

Half Diet Coke, Half Cherry Limeade

A few years ago my aunt Diane was in a car accident. It wasn't her fault, a young guy hit her.

Folks gathered around to see if they could help. Then a young lady who works at Sonic came up to Aunt Diane and said, "I know you. You are the half diet coke, half cherry limeade lady!" As much pain as aunt Diane was in, she had to laugh at that.

It's more Sanitary to Eat at Home
Mom and my cousin, Susie Lacy, were going to the Arkansas Ladies Retreat at the campground. Susie was going to ride with mom.

When Susie arrived at mom's house, she asked mom, "Jessie, are we going to get something to eat along the way? I'm a little bit hungry."

Mom answered, "Susie, why don't I make us a tuna fish sandwich and we'll eat here? Besides, when you eat at a restaurant, you never know if your food is going to be dirty or not. No telling how many bugs get dropped in the soup!"

As they were sitting around the table eating their sandwich, Susie reached up and began to pull something out of her mouth. What on earth was it!

Susie said, "Jessie! This is the wrapper tie from the bread!" they began to laugh as they thought about mom's statement about the cleanliness of restaurants!

A Funny Halloween
A funny thing happened to me last Halloween. I hid the Butter Fingers (duh!) and had the taffy candy ready to give out. Then it dawned on me, "I have two hand-fulls of granny-candy (peppermints, red and white stripped) and I'll get rid of them first."

So by the second round of trick-or-treaters, I still had a good handful of them left. As I put them into the little boy's bag, (he was about seven) to my surprise he said, "Is peppermint all you got lady?!"

He took me by surprise and all I could say was, "You're supposed to be thankful!" When he left, I closed the door and belly-laughed at the look on his face. Of course he could have laughed at the look on my face too!

Wet Cement

When I was about ten-years-old, some of us kids went blackberry picking. They grew rampant in Hoopa. My brother, Rick, the pastor's daughter, Scharlene, and a church friend, Larry, had our own gallon buckets and we filled them up with huge blackberries.

Then we went door to door in an effort to sell them. We were not having much success. Then we came up to a newly built house. I was the youngest, so they had me knock on the door.

But as I stepped onto the sidewalk, I felt myself sink into it. I had stepped in wet, fresh cement! Rick, Scharlene and Larry ran away leaving me all alone.

I knew I needed to tell someone what I had done. So I walked around to the back of the house and knocked on that door.

A man answered, "Yes, can I help you little girl?"

"I stepped in your wet cement out front. I didn't know it was wet. I'm very sorry sir." I said, ending with my head down. "Well, let's go take a look at it." He replied.

He looked at it, then took a trowel and began to smooth it out. "With as hot as it is today, this would have been impossible to fix right in about another hour. I sure thank you for coming and telling me." He was a kind man! AND! He bought my blackberries!

That night at church, during testimony service, Brother Eastburn stood to testify. He was a member there and was like a grandfather to me. He also worked as a door to door salesman.

He began with, "Today I was at a new home making a sale when Kay came and knocked on the backdoor. She told the man that she had stepped in his wet cement. The man fixed it and when he came back into the house, he said that was a nice little girl to come and tell me what she had done. Most kids would have run off." Then he glanced over at Rick, Scharlene and Larry. He continued, "I was so proud to tell him that Kay went to my church."

You will never know how happy I was that day that I didn't run away. If it had been another day, I probably would have! After all, I'm not an angel!

The Visit to my Dentist

I went to the dentist; they placed me in a room. Soon, doctor Beeson came and gave me a shot. He then left to give it time to deaden.

In the meantime, I needed to use the restroom. Afterwards, I came back and sat in the chair. I was waiting for what seemed a very long time. I began to think, if he doesn't hurry up, I will need another shot!

Then he came and stood at the door and asked me if I was ready. I said, "I sure am". He then responded, "Okay, then why don't you come and get back in the room we had you in?" Then he laughed and told me I was in the wrong room. I was in room number 2, but had been assigned to room number 3. They were wondering where I was, and I was wondering where they were!

My dentist also said that I made a very good impression! Get it?

The Pharmacy

My friend, Susan Lowry and I went to Winn Dixie one day. I told her while she was grocery shopping, I needed to talk to the Pharmacist.

I walked up to the pharmacy counter and began to tell this young black lady about my problem. She said, "Girl, my mother was bothered with that once. I feel for you." I had only just met her, but I loved that girl! She was full of compassion!

I asked, "What did your mother do about it?" She replied, "I really do not remember." I proceeded in conversation, "Well, what do you recommend?" She answered, "I really don't have any idea as to what to do." Hmm, I thought. What kind of pharmacy is this anyway?

About that time, Susan came running over to me and said, "Kay, this is not the pharmacy! It's the cigarette counter!" I looked up and saw a sign that read, "*PHARMACY*". As I noticed shelf after shelf of cigarettes behind the lady, I inquired, "Why is that sign there?"

She told me that it was to point people to the pharmacy *around the corner*. I thought, "Well, why don't they put an arrow on it then!"

As we left the store, we were laughing so hard we could hardly walk! When we got in the car, Larry and Justin said, "What have you two done this time?"

Rocky Mount. Virginia

Brother and Sister Graham had invited me to come preach a revival at Rocky Mount, Virginia. I had never been there before, so I put the address into my GPS.

I arrived about 10:30 that Sunday morning. I don't know why I think I have to carry everything in one load, but I do. I was carrying my guitar, guitar stand, briefcase, bag of CD's and my purse. I felt like a pack mule!

As I approached the double-glass front door, I reached to open it and noticed it said, "Jehovah Witness Church". Well, since they were not expecting me, I turned with all of my paraphernalia under my arms, and loaded it back in my car.

As I drove out of the parking lot, I looked straight across the street, and there it was, the Church of God of Prophecy! When I told the congregation what I had done, they had a good laugh.

But! I'm not the only minister that has done this. I won't call anyone's name because you know who you are, Brother and Sister Davis!

Kay, Age 5

CHAPTER 11
KIDS! I LOVE 'EM!

Quinton

Quinton is my nephew. All of the stories that are written here, are when he was between the ages of four and five.

I had been gone in revivals for five weeks and had just gotten home. I decided to pull a trick on Quinton. It was a Saturday and I called Margie to tell her what I was going to do.

I asked to speak with Quinton. I told him I would be gone for five more weeks. He was sad as I told him, "But if I were there, I'd kiss your ears off".

I was standing at their front door as I was speaking to him. I rang the doorbell and Margie asked him to get it. He was still on the phone with me and said, "Kay-Kay, someone is at the door."

I said, "You better answer it then". He opened the door and there I stood with the phone in my hand! Then, I kissed his ears off.

Speaking of kissing ears off, last year a friend of mine in Pocahontas, Arkansas, e-mailed me and said her son (who is now grown) made mention of me the other day about kissing his ears off. That is something I have done for decades to kids, and they seem to love it.

In fact, just yesterday I was at Ian's house (Ian is Lois's grandson). Ian is four-years-old. I have known him since the day he was born to Danielle and David Blanton.

I was getting ready to go home when Ian exclaimed, "Kay-Kay, you forgot to kiss my ears off!" So, I wrestled him down and kissed his ears off. They also have a year-old daughter, Ava. She doesn't know it yet, but soon she'll be asking me to kiss her ears off!

Back to Quinton

It was around Christmastime and Quinton had a decision to make, spend the night with his aunt Kay-Kay or go duck hunting with his Dad.

He thought a minute and said, "I want to spend the night with you Kay-Kay. I'd rather see you than a *dead duck* any ole day!" I tried really hard to take that as a compliment.

Then there was the time I sent Quinton money to take his Mama out for Mother's Day. When it came, he proudly told his mom, "Mama, you can pick where we get to eat. So, do you want to eat at McDonald's, Burger King, or Wendy's?" Happy Mother's Day, Margie!

I Know How to Hypnotize

While visiting at Margie's house, Quinton and I went in the backyard and were playing with his dog, Susie Q. We later came inside and he said, "Kay Kay, swing me." I said, "Quinton, this living room is too little for me to swing you in."

He crawled up onto my lap and said, "Do you want to see my new trick?" I told him yes. He said, "OK, I will be right back, you stay there."

He came back, crawled up in my lap and said, "I know how to hypnotize you." I answered, "You do? Go ahead".

He had brought with him a gold coin looking token. He held it in front of my eyes and moved it from left to right and said, "You are being hypnotized, you are being hypnotized."

I followed along with him and said in a sleepy voice, "What do I do when you hypnotize me?" He said, "Whatever I tell you to do. Hit yourself in the head." With that command, I reached up and hit myself in the head.

Then he said something that Margie and I was not expecting. Still moving the coin in front of my eyes he said, "Now, you will swing me."

Margie and I started laughing uncontrollably. I thought to myself, he is a chip off his Auntie Kay-Kay's block!

You Get Paid?

When Quinton was about four-years old, he asked me why I was gone so much of the time. I told him that I was an Evangelist and traveled around the United States preaching.

Still a little confused, he asks, "What do you do? Do you talk?"

"Yes Quinton, I talk to the people" I replied.

"You mean, they actually *PAY* you to talk!" he exclaimed. He left me speechless, which is hard to do!

I saw Jesus

Ian and I were on our way to Wal-Mart to get some donuts. We love donuts! As we passed a graveyard with lots of flowers in it, Ian said, "Papa took me there to see Jesus".

I thought maybe he had gone to see one of his relatives who had passed away. So I asked him, "Who did you see?"

"I saw Jesus, Kay-Kay!" he replied. I said, "Oh, you saw Jesus at the graveyard?" He said, "No, I saw Jesus in the flower yard!" I thought, well, with so many flowers, it could be called a flower yard!

Beat by an Old Lady!

During a revival, The Sedwick's grand-children were visiting that Sunday afternoon. After dinner I played pool with the two brothers, ages six and eight.

During the game, the eight year old, Zack said, "Miss Kay, how old are you?" I told him I was 50 (at that time, I was).

He replied, "You look a lot younger than you really are!" I tried not to laugh while thanking him.

I won the first game and Zack won the second game. The heat was on for the third game. When I won that game, Zack laid his pool stick down and exclaimed, "Man! I've been beat by an old lady!" It's funny how I went from, "You look a lot younger than you really are" to "Beat by an old lady!" Kids, I love 'em!

Adies

In a revival in Virginia, I asked a little eight-year-old girl where the ladies restroom was. She responded, "Through that door to the left. But, the "L" fell off and now it only says "adies". She was so serious.

A Six-Year-Olds Perspective

While visiting in Virginia, I had preached at a little country church. There was only one child there that morning. I was given the pulpit at 11:40 and had to say what I had, in a hurry. Well, people were at the altar for a long time and service was not over until 12:30.

I was greeting all the people as they were leaving. When I came to this little six-year-old girl, I asked her the normal questions you ask a six-year-old, name, age and when her birthday was. After the interrogation was over, she had a question for me.

She said, "Do you know that when you were up there talking, that you were up there for a *really long time?*" I laughed so hard and said, "Yes honey I did." Kids, I love 'em!

Dang!

I had a new experience while preaching a revival in Sterling, Georgia, where Brother J.W. Griffin is the pastor.

The church was pretty full because Pastor Randy Dockery from Saint Marys was there with a lot of his members.

I was making a comparison about weight. I said, "For example, if I put five pounds a month on, in a year's time, I will weigh sixty pounds more."

A little five-year-old boy yelled out, "DANG!"

The church burst out in laughter as I said, "Well, at least I know I have his attention!"

Boot Scootin' Boogie

One Sunday I was preaching at Friendship, Arkansas, where I was pastoring. All the kids were sitting on the front pew. Tyler was being his usual hyper self and was down in the floor playing. I said, "Tyler, get up, turn around and sit down."

Caleb was sitting beside him and began to sing, "And do the boot scootin' boogie." That was the end of service. We all laughed so hard.

That was a very popular song at that time. Lots of good memories through the years. Tyler turned out to be a very good looking young man! He is a Chiropractor, and is just as calm as can be!

From 0 to 60 in a Second!

While in revival in Mid West City, Oklahoma, I was staying in Darrell and Jana Phillips home. Their son Dayton was just a baby. Jana was sitting in the floor at the end of the treadmill holding him.

All of a sudden, their three-year-old daughter, Dakota climbed on to the treadmill. She reached up and grabbed the knob, spun it to high throwing her feet out from under her. She shot out like a bullet, right into Jana's lap. So now Jana had two children in her lap! You should have seen Dakota's eyes, big as a saucer! By the way, Dakota graduates from college in December!

Fast Forward a Few Years When It Just Wasn't the Right Time

I was winding my message down at Worstell, Oklahoma, where Darrell and Jana Phillips Pastor. I was ready to give the altar call. I stepped off the platform and walked to the right of the congregation. The Spirit was right and I was ready.

All of a sudden the pastor's little five-year old, Dayton holds some pictures out to give me that he had cut out, and *yells*, "Here Kay-Kay, I cut you out some sermon illustrations!"

I knew better than to look at him, or to respond to him. So I just walked over to the other side of the congregation. His Dad was giving him the *"evil eye"* as his Mom was quietly taking the *illustrations* from his hands. Everyone wanted to laugh, but knew it just wasn't *the right time!*

Brain Freeze

During a revival in Oklahoma, the pastor's five-year old son was a bit *active* before church started. So to head off any *extra activity*, I said to him, "I really would appreciate it if you would be good while I am preaching. Could you do that for Sister Kay?"

He thought for a moment and then replied, "Sure I can!" Then I saw a look come over his face and knew he had another thought. He then said, "That is unless I have a brain freeze, then I can't help it." I had to walk away...

Caleb and the Black Bear!

I was visiting some friends in Rogers, Arkansas. Their seven year-old son wanted to ride with me from the store to their house.

It was dark as we pulled up to the house. He said, "I sure hope mom and dad hurry and get here because I need to go to the bathroom bad!"

I told him that he could go around the corner of the house and go if he wanted to. He thought that sounded like a great idea.

Then I said, "I sure hope that black bear doesn't get you." He said, "What bear!" I told him that one got away from the zoo. He said, "Well, if he is from the zoo, he is probably a friendly bear."

Holding a straight face, I replied, "He has already eaten three kids today. But, I'll tell you what I'll do. If I see him coming, I will honk the horn and you come a running!" He agreed.

When I figured he was finished doing *his job*, I honked the horn. He came running and jumped in my car and said, "Kay-Kay, *you* didn't scare me, but whatever was in that bush sure did!!!"

I began laughing, and then told him that there really wasn't a bear on the loose.

Remedy for Sleepless Nights

My cousin Gayle called to tell me about her granddaughter, Callie. Gayle uses my singing CD to put her to sleep. She said that when Callie is fighting sleep, she will ask her, "Do you want to listen to Kay?" She will say, "No Kay, no Kay!"

Gayle told me when Callie listens to my CD, she always falls asleep! So sometimes Gayle doesn't ask her, and puts in on anyway. Callie goes right to sleep listening to me sing.

But when she was having a hard time going to sleep, she'd say Kaayyyy!!!! So I guess if you are having trouble going to sleep, just put my CD on! I just pray that my preaching doesn't have the same effect!

Movies Rated by a 7 year old

Clay and Brandy Clark's son, C.J. was discussing movie ratings. He said, "Mom, G is for everyone. PG is parental guidance. PG13 is for 13 and older. R is for 18 or older. X? X rated must be for senior citizens!"

Not Bored

A young lady attended my revival for the first time. She had been on drugs for years and had been *clean* for six months.

At the close of service, she testified and said, "I loved the service tonight. I was not bored and my butt is not sore!" Well, I thought that was quite a compliment! Young people, I just love 'em!

Board Members

At the close of his sermon, the pastor made this announcement. "I would like to see all the board members in my office."

Immediately a lady got up and headed towards his office. He asked her, "Where are you going?" To which she replied, "I am probably the most *bored* member in this church!"

Looks like that tree might just fall on me. It's being held up by a block of wood!

Chapter 12
I HAVE CRAZY FRIENDS

Hello Norma

Henry and Norma Schneider used to pastor the church at Hill Haven, Oklahoma. I was in revival there and we were on our way home from church one night. I was in the backseat of their Cadillac and I called her cell phone.

She answered, "Hello". I said, "Hello there! What are you doing?" Unaware that she was talking to me in the backseat, she said, "Henry and I are on our way home. We are in revival." I said, "Really, with who?" She replied, "Sis. Kay Osban, she is from Arkansas. We are having a great revival!"

Henry could see me in his rearview mirror and knew I was playing a joke on Norma. He wanted to laugh so bad!

As we were approaching Yell Avenue, I said, "Norma, are you on Broken Arrow Expressway, about to pass Yell Avenue?" She got really quiet and was wondering how "this person" could know where she was. She finally responded, "Yes, I am." I broke out laughing and said, "So am I. Norma, this is Kay. I'm in the backseat!"

Need I say more...?

Neutered?

In 2006 I was in revival at Trumann, Arkansas. My friends, Janice and Russell Page lived right across the street from the pastor. Russell had just had surgery on his rotor cuff and was off from work.

His mother-in-law, Lorene, had called and needed him to come to her house. Since he was not able to drive, I volunteered to take him.

When we arrived, Lorene told us that her dog, Chi Chi, was not able to walk.

She wanted us to take her dog to the vet. So, with tears in Lorene's eyes, she said goodbye to Chi Chi.

So off to the vet we go, with me driving and Russell holding the dog. As the vet was looking Chi Chi over, she said to (I am going to call them Nurse number one and Nurse number two) nurse number one, "Please go get nurse number two."

As nurse number one exits the room, the lady vet said to us, "She has just had surgery and can't lift anything over five pounds." Well, although Chi Chi was a Chihuahua, she weighed a whopping twenty pounds!

Russell was nervous at the thought of having Chi Chi *put down*. So he struck up a conversation with who he thought was nurse number one (the one who had surgery). He said, "I just had surgery myself. What kind of surgery did you have?"

I thought to myself, he shouldn't ask her that. But she misunderstood him and thought he asked her what kind of surgery she had done that day. So, she replies, "*Neutered*". My head nearly spun off my neck as I looked from him to her.

Russell's next statement let me know just how *out of it* he was. He said, "Were you neutered on your uterus?"

At that moment I thought I would die. Trying to hold in laughter can kill you! Fortunately, nurse number two didn't hear him. Or maybe she didn't understand the question, "Were you neutered on your uterus?" and decided to leave well enough alone.

Well, they put Chi Chi in a box. Russell sat in the back seat and I handed him the *package*. When I got in the drivers seat, I burst out laughing. Russell wanted to know what was so funny. I could hardly tell him between the laughs. I told him that he had asked that lady if she had been neutered.

As I was telling him this, I was looking at him in the rearview mirror. I saw confusion on his face. Then, I saw it. Reality hit him and he had regained his senses.

He said, "Oh no! I even asked her if she had been neutered on her uterus! Oh Lord! Oh Lord! I am never coming back here again!" I said, "And I am never coming back here *with you* again!"

After I dug a hole and buried Chi Chi, I made a mad dash to the school's library to tell his wife Janice. Needless to say, we had a great laugh!

I would like to add a little to this story. Russell and Janice Page have been wonderful friends to me and my family. When mom was dying, they made several trips to the house to pray for her. They always gave daddy all the plums he wanted from their tree. He loved to make plum jelly, and it was plum good!

MAD GOPHER!

While standing at the kitchen window in Guthrie, Oklahoma, Linda Beal noticed dirt flying in the backyard. "Ah ha, that gopher is back! I'll fix him."

She quickly grabbed her box of "mothballs" and out the backdoor she went. She dropped several mothballs down the hole, filled it in and then put a cinder block on top of the mound. "There, that should keep you away".

Later on that day, to her great surprise, she looked and saw where they had dug out of the hole, making a new hole *beside* the cinder block. BUT! Not only had they made a new hole, they had neatly placed all the mothballs around it!

When she told me about it, I said, "Well, I guess that gopher decided if you didn't want him in your backyard, he'd at least give you back your mothballs!"

Later On...

In the front yard, she saw a baby gopher with no hair on it. It had died, so the other gophers pushed it out from under the ground and left it by the side of the hole.

Linda said, "We bury our dead under the ground, while we live above it. But gophers must bury theirs on top of the ground while they live under it." Makes sense to me!

Cinder Blocks

Back in 1990, the church at Hope, Arkansas, was building a new church. We were raising money to build it debt free. At least that was our goal.

We had "White Elephant Auctions", car washes and yard sales. *We the people* worked very hard. We did as much of the work ourselves to save money.

One day Maryann and I were driving to the store, and she saw about a dozen cinder blocks in someone's yard. She said, "Stop Kay!" and I did.

She continued, "Kay, go knock on their door and ask them if we can have those cinder blocks for the church."

"What? You want *me* to just go to their door and ask them?" I replied. I could tell she did. I just love it when someone else feels led for *you* to do something!

So I explained the situation to them and they were glad to get rid of them! We loaded them up and took them to the church.

During this time of building, I think it would have been dangerous to have left anything lying around that we could have used.

But because of all of the hard work, Hope now has a beautiful brick building for folks to worship in.

Coffee Beans?

Donnie ran a food pantry and was always getting things donated to him to help feed the *homeless*. Once he got a lot of *whole* coffee beans. They were in one pound coffee bags. He knew it would be hard for the homeless to grind them, so he gave me a bag of them. I took it with me to Linda's in Oklahoma.

While we were at a grocery store, I asked them if I could use their coffee grinder to grind my coffee beans. They said, "Sure".

So, I ground them all up. I thought they looked a bit strange because they were lightly colored, especially for coffee beans. So I took them to Linda's house.

We were excited about having a cup of fresh brewed coffee! When it was finished, I poured myself a cup, and noticed it was very light in color. I added a spoon of sugar and took a drink.

It was *not* coffee beans! I had ground up a pound of pinto soup beans!!! My next thought was, "What does one do with a pound of ground up soup beans!"

I called Donnie, laughing so hard I could barely tell him that he had given me soup beans instead of coffee beans! He thought that since they were in a coffee bag, that it was coffee beans. Go figure!

Earl and Marlene Hulett

When I first came to Saint Marys, Georgia, Earl and Marlene were some of the first ones I met at church. Earl was the usher and we hit it right off. Before he knew who I was, he told Marlene, "I think that lady is a minister, she's crazy!"

They have become some of my best friends. There is no way I could write a chapter about my crazy friends and not write about them!

When we are together, there is a lot of laughter going on. Earl loves for me to sing, "I'm not Crazy" because he knows its not true, for me or him.

As I was writing this book, I spent several nights up until two or three o'clock in the morning trying to get it finished. Earl and Marlene called and said they were going to Chauncey, Georgia, to fish and wanted to know if I wanted to go also.

I wanted to, but knew I had a deadline for this book. I finally decided to go, "I need a break from this" I told myself. I drove up there and I had a blast.

Earl would cast his line in the water and say, "Fish, have you ever heard of the hereafter? Well, I'm here after you!"

Between Earl, Marlene, Mildred (Marlene's sister) and I, we caught about eighty catfish! I felt sorry for Earl, he had to clean all of them.

Once I was running a little late to meet them at their house. When I arrived, I began to give an excuse as to what happened to make me late.

I'll never forget what Earl said, "Poor planning on your part doesn't make it an emergency on my part!" Marlene is my friend and Earl is my buddy!

Saint Marys, Georgia, Church of God of Prophecy

When I moved to Saint Marys in 2009, I was thankful for a great local church that I could attend while I would be home from revivals. Brother Randy Dockery is the Pastor. He is a great Pastor and is willing to help anyone at any time. He has a heart for Jesus!

I Don't Want Any!!

Speaking of the Saint Marys church, Lois and I had been hired to paint the house across the street from the church. Pastor Randy had brought all the paint over and got us all set up.

He visited for a few moments, told us to lock the front door, and walked back over to the church. I was busy painting one of the bedrooms, when I heard the doorbell ring.

"Lois," I said, "he has forgotten something."

I climbed down off the ladder and went to the door. On the way to the door, I thought of something funny to do. I slung the door open with force and yelled, "Whatever you've got, I don't want any!"

To my great surprise, there stood two black gentlemen with a Bible under their arms. They were there to witness to me about Jehovah! Their eyes grew really big as they said, "You don't want any of Jesus?"

I began to apologize and try to explain that I was trying to play a trick on my pastor, who was across the street. They began to laugh; thank God they had a sense of humor!

We watched as their van came to pick them up, there were several people in the van. Before they got in, they began to tell the experience of what had just happed to them at *that* house. They all burst into laughter. The next time I have a bright idea, I believe I'll peek out the window first!

The Smoke is Getting Thicker

I was staying with Dennis and Linda McLemore during my revival at North Tazewell, Virginia. Brother Dennis is the pastor.

We had planned a catfish dinner for about ten of us. I fried it all up, and we sat down for the feast! About thirty minutes into the meal, I smelt smoke.

Linda jumped up and she and I ran to the oven. When she opened the oven door, black smoke bellowed out! I had seen something like this on TV before, but never in real life!

It was a piecrust she had put in just before we had sat down to eat. She only wanted to brown it a tad. Well, it was a tad too brown, it was as black as coal.

Being the merciful person I am, (ha!) I went to my room and wrote a song about it. We snuck the piecrust into the church, and as their granddaughter, Kaitlin brought the piecrust out, I sang this song.

LINDA TURNED 65,
NOW, WHEN SHE BAKES A PIE,
THE FIRE DEPARTMENT WILL ARRIVE.
THE CRUST IS AS BLACK AS NIGHT,
CRUST IS SUPPOSED TO BE LIGHT,
LINDA YOU AIN'T RIGHT!
I SAID "SOMETHING IS BURNING"
SO TO THE OVEN LINDA WENT RUNNING!
BUT IT WAS TOO LATE.
WE WERE ABOUT TO MEET OUR FATE!
SMOKE BELLOWED OUT SO THICK,
I HAD BEEN GETTING WELL, BUT ONCE, AGAIN I'M SICK!
WE HAVE A LOT TO BE THANKFUL FOR,
THERE'S STILL A HOUSE STANDING,
AT THE MCLEMORE'S!

The great thing about the North Tazewell church is they know how to have fun, but they also have some of the most powerful services as well!

They also have two members there, Charles and Diana Heldreth. It's so neat to be able to say that I had dinner with Charles and Diana!

I must tell this about Brother McLemore or bust! Years ago he was outside on a ladder painting. Somehow he managed to lose his footing and fell.

But his foot got hung on the ladder rung and he found himself hanging upside down! Their youngest daughter, Beth, was still living at home.

He hollered and hollered for her. Finally, she heard him and came a running. When she got outside, she found her dad hanging upside down. He asked her to go get the neighbor to help him. And she did.

When they told me this story, I thought I would never stop laughing! Dennis wears a mustache. He jokingly told me he wears a mustache because he never wants to be accused of being a bald-faced liar!

Yard Sale

I have a friend who loves to go to yard sales. She was at this one house looking though all the stuff when a lady asked if she could help her.

My friend held up an item and said, "Yes, how much do you want for this?" The lady responded, "It's not for sale. I have dragged all this stuff out of my garage so I could clean it out. This is not a yard sale."

When you Cry Fox

It was April Fools day and I was having a ball. Six of us ladies were on our way to the Georgia Ladies Retreat. Marlene, Mildred, Marty, Barbara, Lois and I stopped for lunch and I continued to pull pranks and saying, "April Fools!"

Mrs. Marty had just about had enough and said, "Kay, one of these days you are going to cry *Fox* and no one is going to come running!"

I just looked at her and said one word, *Wolf*. The whole table exploded into laughter. The expression on her face was priceless. She will always cry *wolf* from now on and not *fox*!

I miss Marty and her husband, Reggie Whitehurst. They were always doing for others. Reggie could fix about anything. He has fixed a lot of stuff here at my house. They moved to Mississippi.

That's just Funny

Have you ever wondered about things? I mean, inquiring minds want to know! For instance, did Adam and Eve have a bellybutton? Think about it!

Why would my friend, Dot Watson, who by the way is in her eighties, send me a pair of underwear that is a size 100?! She sent those to me last Christmas! They were even the holiday color, red. That lady is a mess! She reminds me a lot of my Granny James.

And why would an owner call his bar, "The Rehab Saloon"? I guess because they all seek advice from the bartender!

I have a friend who's last name was Bean before she married a Rice. She went from a Bean to a Rice!

Another friend's last name was Freeze and she married a Frost. She went from a Freeze to a Frost!

Sheets, Oh Sheets! Where Are You?

My friends, Geary and Dianne Jonas pastor in Virginia. While in revival at their church, they told me this story. I had a good laugh from it! I ask Dianne to write it for me, so here it is!

"My husband is a Pastor, and we had invited an Evangelist for revival. He held a five night revival.

The night he left, I went into the bedroom where he slept to change the sheets. To my surprise there were *no sheets* on the bed to take off. I thought that he had put them in the clothes hamper. They were not there. I went down to the laundry room. There were *no sheets* there.

My daughter and her boyfriend were sitting on the couch. He could see I was frantically looking for something. He asked if I had lost something. I said, "There are no sheets on the bed!"

By this time I was grasping at straws. I asked my husband if he had taken them off, knowing that he had not. He said, "I will just call him." They talked a few minutes and then he asked him, "Those five nights you stayed with us, were there any pillowcases on the pillows?" He said, "No sir." "Were there any sheets on the bed?"

"No sir," he replied.

He said, "Why didn't you tell us?" The Evangelist stated that he just slept on top of the bedspread, as it was during the summer months. I have never been so embarrassed in my life! I just sat down in my recliner and did not do a single thing the rest of the evening.

We did invite him again for revival, and guess what? He came! It was very hard for me to look him in the eye after what I had done. But believe me, I checked the bed several times before he came back to make sure there were sheets on the bed!

I learned a lesson the hard way. Never take the sheets off the bed and just pull the blanket and bedspread up and think, I'll put the sheets on later.

We invited another Evangelist and his wife for revival. They knew about this story. When they came to the door, she asked, "Do I need to bring my sheets in?"

*In over 30 years of being on the Evangelistic field, I can say I've never encountered *no sheets*!

Red Hat Convention!

The Gas Light is Shinning Brighter!

I left St. Marys, Georgia, October 7, 2010 heading to Max Meadows, Virginia, for their second annual Ladies Night Out. Lois was with me and we were to be at the pastors house (Brother and Sister Jonas) that evening. Everything was going well until the traffic came to a stop on I-26 in S.C., nearly into N.C.

It was 4p.m. and we thought it would only be a short delay. Then we found out that there had been an accident that morning at 9:00 and that the interstate would be closed until midnight! The GPS told us the next exit was seven miles ahead. That is where they were having everyone to exit. We had a quarter of a tank of gas, no worries right? Wrong!

An hour later of inching along, the gas light came on. We had hardly moved. I called 911 and asked if I could drive on the shoulder to the exit because I was running out of gas. "No!" was her reply. I wanted to tell her that I had already seen about twenty-five cars do that, but I refrained.

About that time we saw a van driving rather fast on the shoulder of the road *MEETING* us! They had turned around to go back to the last exit! As they drew closer, I noticed it was a van full of women, church women!

It had the name of their church on the side of the van. The lady driving had a death grip on the steering wheel and the others looked rather pale. That gave us the laugh of the day!

So there we sat, hungry. We had begun a diet two days earlier, so I knew we had not packed any candy bars or snacks. BUT! We did have sunflower seeds! We were eating them and enjoying them so much. There is something about eating sunflower seeds though, they make you thirsty. Now, we had plenty of water, and we were really drinking it.

Three hours later, we needed to use the bathroom; of course there wasn't one in sight. So we put the seeds away and prayed that the traffic would move a little faster.

Men began to pull off the shoulder onto the grass, park their vehicle and run up the embankment into the woods. Lois looked at me and said, "I wonder what they are doing?" I explained to her that the whole world was the men's bathroom. "Oh," she said. I looked over at her and there she was just a gawking! Not really!

Four hours later, we really need to go! The gas light is shining brighter, especially since it is now dark! We see a Shell gas station light shining in the distance. It took another 30 minutes to get to it.

Then we noticed that the police cars were everywhere at the exit, and had it blocked off so you could only turn right. If I turned right, I would be going *away* from the gas station!

Looking to the right, all you could see was a sea of taillights! I knew God had helped us not to run out of gas. It had been a miracle for the past three and a half hours that the light was on not to run out. But this would have been pushing it to try to go on any further without getting gas.

So I did turn right, then immediately did a u-turn and headed for that Shell station. Lois said, "You can't do that! There are policemen everywhere!" I told her we had to. I was not going to run out of gas at 9:00 at night, especially when there was a station right there.

We bought gas and bought some snacks. The snacks were so very stale! A couple told us about a short cut on 321. So when I paid for the snacks, I asked the lady behind the counter, "So, tell me, how do you get to highway 321?" She told me to take a right out of the station and then take the first right, then another right..." and so on.

So, I did as she said and ten minutes later I topped a hill and there it was, that same Shell station! I was so aggravated by this time that I turned around. Lois knew I was not a happy camper, so she began singing, "This is the day that the Lord has made. I will rejoice and be glad in it."

Then she looked my way and saw that I was glaring at her. And she immediately said, "Or, maybe not."

We finally found the shortcut and got back on the right road, far ahead of the sea of taillights. We were so happy. Needless to say we didn't make it to the pastor's house. We didn't think they would want us showing up at 3:00 in the morning. So, Tom Bodett left the light on for us at Motel 6!

The next day, I asked Lois to drive because I felt a song coming on. This is what I wrote and sang that night for the ladies.

ON OUR WAY HERE (Written by Kay Osban Oct. 8, 2010)
(To the tune of "Happy Trails to You")

On our way here, as happy as could be.
Until the traffic stopped, as far as the eye could see.
Thought it would be a quick delay,
Didn't know that it would be all day.
On our way here,
Max Meadows is no where near!
Gas light began to shine, my nerves began to grind!
The light was oh so bright.
Much brighter now that it's night!
I'd really like to see a Hilton
Wait! Up there I think I see a buildin'
It's Tom Bodett I see,
He's left the light on for me!!!

Krispy Kreme Queen

When I am in revival at Clay Hill, Florida, (where Bishop Billy Canterbury is the pastor;) the members call me their Krispy Kreme Queen. The reason being is they found out how much I love those donuts!

This year, at the close of the revival, they presented me with a ceramic piggy bank. It was in the shape of three donuts stacked on top of each other! They looked good enough to eat.

They had filled it full of coins, one hundred dollars in coins! We always conclude the revival with a dinner afterwards. Along with the ceramic donuts, they gave me a dozen Krispy Kreme donuts. Clay Hill really knows how to party!

Brother and Sister Murphy

I was in revival at Huddleston, Virginia. At that time brother Murphy was the pastor. He and sister Murphy took me to the Peaks of Otter on the Blue Ridge Parkway. It was in the Fall and the leaves were absolutely beautiful. On the way, we stopped by and got their daughter, Waylene.

After we ate, on the way back home I asked Bro. Murphy to stop at these beautiful trees with their gorgeous yellow and orange leaves. He did and I took pictures of the three of them standing by the trees.

I then said, "Bro. Murphy, Waylene and I are going to walk down the road to that pullover spot. There is a huge rock there and I want to take Waylene's picture sitting on it. You and Sis. Murphy can drive down there and pick us up." He agreed.

So, with my back to the road and Waylene sitting on the rock, I began taking a multitude of pictures. The Murphy's have a red van, and in the corner of my eye I saw the red van drive onto the pullover, and then begin to ease on out onto the road.

Now, if you know Bro. Murphy, you know he is a prankster. I knew what he was doing, he was acting like he was going to run off and leave us.

So, with the camera to my right eye, and viewing the van pulling out with my left eye, (by the way, this tends to make one "cockeyed") I pointed my left hand at the van and said (with much authority in my voice) "You pull that van over right now!!!" And he did, and stopped.

Then within thirty seconds another red van pulled in behind that red van. Waylene began to laugh hysterically. She realized I had told a total stranger to pull his van over... and he did!

When the first van saw the second van pull in behind him, I think he realized that "I" had made a mistake and he drove on, probably laughing his head off.

Waylene and I walked to Bro. Murphy's van laughing as we went. They wanted to know what was so funny. When we told them, he laughed and shook his head in disbelief.

At church that night, he asked me to come to the pulpit, handed me the microphone and told me to tell the congregation what I had done that day.

Who's going to Drive?

Dan and Minnie Teeter are very good friends of mine from Russellville, Arkansas. Minnie owned and ran a Preschool and Daycare called "Teeter Totter". Cute, huh? She and Dan both are now retired.

One day Minnie went to pick a child up from school. She put him in the backseat of her minivan and buckled him in. Then she proceeded to the *passenger's* front seat, got in and buckled up.

This perplexed the little boy who finally spoke up and said, "Mrs. Teeter, who's going to drive?"

Minnie realized what she had done, and that she was in the wrong seat. She certainly didn't want him to know that she was out-of-it! So, being the cool person she is, she replied, "Well, I am!"

She got out just as calm as a cucumber, and got in the drivers seat! I think maybe that was one of those days that one too many kids got to her!

I've Never Driven this Before
    I used to stay with the Teeters while in revival at London, Arkansas, (I can say I've been to London!). The church had a bus that they used to carry kids to church with.
    They had lettering painted on it from a design shop. They called and said it was ready. Minnie and I went to pick it up. As I was walking towards it to drive it back to the house, there were some men standing in the parking lot.
    Their trucks were parked a little too close to the bus for my comfort. They had this look on their face like, "I wonder how she is going to get that bus out without hitting one of our trucks?"
    Since they were not offering to move them, I turned to Minnie and said in a rather loud voice, "I've never driven a bus before, but I'll give it a try!"
    Suddenly, they jumped to their feet and ran to their trucks and began moving them. It was amazing how fast the parking lot was cleared! Minnie and I have laughed about that for years!

SNAKE!
    When I was Director of Junior Camp in Arkansas, Dan Teeter was always on my staff. I felt like I had the best staff in the whole wide world! Because, I really did!
    One day a camper ran up to me and said she saw a snake at the putt-putt golf course. She was scared to death. Snakes were very common on the campgrounds. After all, they were there first!
    I called on my buddy, Dan to retrieve the critter. Come to find out, Dan was not fond of snakes either. As he was bent over looking for the snake, I took a stick and touched his ankle with it.

Wow! I didn't know Dan could jump that high! Who would have thought it? I also didn't know he could run that fast as he was chasing me all the way up the hill! He caught me and grabbed a shovel... and that's all I'm going to say about this story!

Brother Skaggs

I was in revival in Mena, Arkansas, where Brother Frank and Sister Pauline Skaggs were pastoring. His mother-in-law was moving next door to them.

I was helping Brother Skaggs unload the truck. When the refrigerator was placed in the right spot in the kitchen, Brother Skaggs reached down to plug it in.

As he was putting the plug into the receptacle, I grabbed his ankle and made a noise like someone was being electrocuted, zzzzz.

Wow! Who knew he could jump like that too! When he figured out it was me, he turned and said, "Sister Kay! You scared me!" I took my ole bad self back to his house where Sister Skaggs and I had a good laugh!

Being Chased with a Broom

That same week, Debbie Skaggs and I went four-wheeler riding. We both had our own four-wheeler, I mean they both belonged to brother Skaggs.

Since I was the new kid on the block, not knowing where we could ride, I was following Debbie.

She drove into this driveway that was "U" shaped, easy in, and right back out. Well, Debbie made it just fine. But as I pulled in I was met by an elderly lady with a broom! She had the broom in both hands and over her head. She was headed right for me as she was yelling, "Get out of my driveway!"

I outran her and got clean out of Dodge! As Debbie was looking back at me, I could see her laughing, laughing hysterically!

I had lunch with Debbie recently and we still laugh about that day!

Smell Phone

Wilma Gentle accidentally called me from her cell phone. Evidently she had pushed my number on speed dial as she sat on the commode at a gas station. When I answered, all I heard was bathroom noise, then water running in a sink.

When her phone finally hung up, I called her back. I said, "Wilma, where are you?" She replied, "At a gas station." I asked, "Did you just come out of the restroom?" By now I picture her looking up in the sky for the satellite that had taken her picture coming out of the restroom.

She very slowly says, "Yes..." I then told her that I had heard the whole episode and that it was so real that I could even smell it. Without missing a beat, she says, "Oh, so you have a smell phone!" Boy, she's quick!

Fat Chance of That Happening!

November 2000 I boarded a very small airplane in Memphis, on my way to speak at a Ladies Retreat. I was seated in the front row, by the door.

The flight attendant was short, but a bit on the *hefty* side. She came up to me and said, "Since you are sitting by the door, there are a few things I need to go over with you."

"First of all, if the plane goes down (I didn't like the thought of that already!) and I become *incapacitated*, (my eye's got bigger) it will be *your responsibility* to see to it that I am *carried* off this plane."

I looked at her and said, "Yes Ma'am". As she was walking away, I said under my breath, *"Fat chance of that happening*! It's everyone for themselves lady!" Thankfully, we arrived just fine!

Place Your Feet Right Here

I was visiting Jeannie and Larry Cossey in Harrisburg, Arkansas. It was a cold wintry day. I had spent the night with them. The next morning the fire had gone out in the woodstove.

Since Larry was at work, I told Jeannie that I could start a fire. There wasn't any kindling split and I told her that I could split some as I grew up cutting wood. Wood is the only heat I knew until I moved to Arkansas.

She was watching me split it all up. She said she was really impressed. I told her, "I can show you how to do it". She said, "Oh no! Larry told me never to touch that axe!"

I coached her on by saying, "Come on Jeannie, I'll show you exactly how to do this. There is nothing to it, watch." So I began cutting bigger pieces of wood into.

I sat a chunk upon the block and said, "Come here Jeannie. Put your feet exactly where my footprints are." She carefully placed her feet in my footprints.

"Now, raise the axe over your head and come down with all your might!" I said.

She did it just the way I showed her. With all the strength she could muster up, she came down with a mighty blow!

When the axe came down, the axe handle is the only part that hit the wood, the axe head was on the other side of the wood. I forgot that Jeannie is taller than me, and her arms are longer! I forgot to make allowance for that.

Poor Jeannie, she looked as though she was in pain! The only way I can explain to you the way she looked, was picture Wiley Coyote standing there shaking in one spot. The axe handle was still, but she was still vibrating!

Now we know why Larry had forbid her to touch the axe. Ya think? There was no hiding it from him either. Jeannie's hands and wrists were all swollen. BUT! The house was warm!

Forty-five Pound Spoonbill!

Whenever I have a revival in Joplin, Missouri, I always stay with Gerald and Shirley Tucker. They own an Elk Ranch and are very good friends.

Once I went there on vacation to go fishing with them. We were fishing on Grand Lake in Oklahoma, which wasn't too far from Carthage, Missouri, where they live.

Grand Lake has some huge spoonbill fish in it. I latched on to one that weighed forty-five pounds! The line was zinging from my reel. The fight was on!

At one point, the fish gave a might tug and I almost flew out of the boat! I probably would have if Gerald hadn't reacted quickly when he saw what was going on.

He looped his finger through the back loop of my jeans and kept me from going overboard. He pulled me to a sitting position where I could brace my feet against the boat.

After wrestling that fish for quite a while, I finally landed it! Gerald really enjoyed telling everyone at church (or wherever) of how he rescued me that day! Man, catching that fish was a lot of fun!

Life Through the Eyes of a Red Headed, Wide-eyed, Full Time Evangelist!

45 Pound Spoonbill

Which Eye?

While on the Elk Farm, one day Shirley and I were going to go shopping. Gerald came in and said someone had bought one of the elk for butcher. Gerald was going to kill and dress it.

"Can I shoot it?" I asked. He asked me if I knew how. I told him that I was a good shot. He did not believe me, so he stuck a 2"x2" piece of paper on a tree and told me to hit it. I shot it dead center.

So, Gerald, Shirley and one of their workers and I went to the field where all the elk were standing. He said, "Kay, do you see those three elk standing off by themselves? Shoot the one in the middle. And if you miss, or maimed it, and I have to run all over this field chasing it, I'll whoop you!"

I assured him I wouldn't do that. He told me the best place to kill them instantly, was to shoot them in the eye. Jokingly I said, "Which eye do you want me to hit?" He said, "I think I'll be happy if you just hit it!" I could tell his confidence in me was low.

I positioned the rifle, stead, aim, fire! I got him, and he was down! The worker drove the forklift over to him as the three of us ran out to see. I had shot him in the left eye.

The worker looked at me and said, "Good shot ma'am!" I felt like Sarah Palin as I walked away. Gerald hollered, "Get back here Kay! Now you've got to clean it". I kept walking as I shouted back, "We're going shopping!" And we did. My mom, a.k.a., Jessie James would have been so proud!

In the Name of Jesus!

I had an experience while visiting my friends, Rhonda and Dewayne Smith in Pocahontas, Arkansas, that I will never forget.

Dewayne's sister, mother, Rhonda and I went to Wal-Mart one day. His sister had just had a baby and asked me to drive. She had an older van and it did not have a keyless entry.

I wanted to go so I could return an item. When we got into the store, I realized that I forgot my sack in the van. I told them I would catch up with them after I got the sack.

It was a cloudy day with drizzling rain. I got to the blue van, stuck the round key in, but it wouldn't unlock. So I stuck the square key in, it still wouldn't unlock.

I was getting aggravated because it was beginning to rain harder, and I had a good hair day and didn't want it messed up! Laugh, but you know its true.

After a few attempts of it not opening, I stopped and as I put the round key in again, I commanded, "Door, in the name of Jesus, you open up!" The lock popped up! Hallelujah!

I got inside and began looking for my sack. It was then that it dawned on me, I am in the wrong van! I was immediately concerned that the owner would find me in there. So I hurried up and got out and locked it back.

I knew I was parked on row seven! I began to walk further down the row and there on the other side of this big dually pickup truck, was her blue van! It opened up with ease.

I began to laugh as I thought about what had happened. I could just see Jesus up there laughing at me. Then when I said, In the name of Jesus, He responded! Be careful what you ask for.

My Beloved Friend, Bill Richardson!

Bill and Judy Richardson pastored in Liberty City, Texas. I conducted several revivals there over the years. I first met them in California when they pastored in Crescent City. That was in the same district as Hoopa was.

They were also Camp Directors when I was a kid. Bill always laughed as he told the congregation that he nicknamed me the Tasmanian devil.

The reason being is, according to him, I would whiz into one place and stir up trouble, then whiz into another place to do the same. I don't remember that. Lol

Bishop Richardson passed from this life to the next in September of 2011. It was so unexpected and hit me hard. Little did I know that three weeks later my dad would pass as well.

Two months later I was back in Liberty City for a revival that Bill had scheduled. His wife stepped in and continued to pastor.

As most everyone knows, I have an "Amen" sign that I carry to every pulpit. When I need an amen, I raise my sign.

When I arrived at the revival, at the front of the church, there in the corner over a door, was an Amen sign. Bill had put it there and had called it his *Amen corner*.

Speaking of Liberty City, there is a member there by the name of Kenneth Collins. He shook my hand and asked me how I was. I told him that if I were any better, I'd be twins. He responded to that with, "Well, if I was any better, I'd feel like it was a frame-up!"

Gregg and Andrea (the Richardson's son-in-law and daughter) were at the revival this year. They have a son and two daughters. Those two girls look so much alike, that I get them mixed up.

Alexis had hurt her foot at school. They had it x-rayed and the doctor said there was a hairline crack. She came to church with a boot.

One night I was praying for everyone at the altar and front pews. I put my hand on her and diligently prayed for God to heal her foot. I was just a praying away! Then she looked up at me and said, "It's my sister's foot that's hurt, not mine." Before I took my hand off of her, I said, "Wrong foot!" Then I went to the next pew and prayed for the right foot!

That child has so much faith that she told her mom. "When I go to the doctor Tuesday, my foot will be alright." Guess what? It was. Isn't that just like our God? Amen!

Foot, Foot Foot and Foot Foot Foot

That last story reminded me of this story that mom used to tell us kids when we were little. Read it, and then try telling it without looking at it.

Once upon a time, there were three little rabbits. Their names were, Foot and Foot Foot, and Foot Foot Foot.

One day Foot and Foot Foot, and Foot Foot Foot were taking a walk in the woods when suddenly Foot hurt his foot.

He cried out, "Oh Foot Foot, and Foot Foot Foot, I've hurt my foot!"

Foot Foot Foot said to Foot Foot, "Foot Foot, go get a doctor for Foot because he hurt his foot." So Foot Foot ran and got a doctor for poor ole Foot.

The doctor said, "Foot Foot and Foot Foot Foot, I'm sorry but poor ole Foot is going to die." So Foot Foot and Foot Foot Foot buried poor ole Foot.

As they were walking back home, Foot Foot cried out to Foot Foot Foot, "Oh! Foot Foot Foot, I've hurt *my* foot!"

Foot Foot Foot said, "Foot Foot, I'll go get a doctor for your hurt foot." So Foot Foot Foot brought back the doctor for poor ole Foot Foot.

The doctor hung his head and said, "Foot Foot Foot, I'm sorry, but Foot Foot is going die." Foot Foot Foot cried out in a loud voice, "No, no! Foot Foot can't die, I've already got one Foot in the grave!!!"

Guest Speaker at Washington's Youth Retreat

CHAPTER 13
MY FAMILY DOESN'T SUFFER FROM INSANITY, WE RATHER ENJOY IT!

Mom and dad were in Arkansas on vacation visiting Wilma and Charlie Gentle, I was there also. We were all going to eat at a really good catfish restaurant.

The restaurant offered an all you can eat catfish buffet. We were, as my uncle Joe Lacy would say, "frogging our sides". The food was wonderful and so was the company.

They had a sign posted on the buffet, "NO SHARING FOOD, AND, DO NOT TAKE ANY HOME WITH YOU".

I had an appointment, so I was the first to leave. Before I left, I wrapped a piece of fish in a napkin and slipped it into mom's jacket pocket.

On my way out, I took the manager aside and told him what I had done. I asked him to confront my mom about it, and then tell her it was all a joke. He was pleased to fill my request! I like a man with a sense of humor.

I hid with great anticipation as I watched this all unfold. He walked to their table and asked if everything was alright. They assured him it was. They were having a great time.

Then he said, "Did you all notice my sign about not sharing or taking any food home?" Confused, they all said they had seen it. He then asked mom to look in her jacket pocket.

With confidence she put her hand in the pocket and pulled out a piece of wrapped up fish. No one was more surprised than mom! She tried to explain, "I don't know how that got in there!" Her next word out of her mouth was, "Kay! My daughter Kay did this!"

The manager began to laugh as he shook his head yes. He told mom that I had put him up to it. As I heard the table burst into laughter, I decided to go ahead and leave.

Playing Church

My cousins and I used to play church all the time. Gayle was four, Kathy was nine and I was six.

I was bossy then, just like I am now. I think I was born bossy. Bossy is such a misunderstood word. We feel we just have better ideas, and that's the only way we know to put it across. Lol

We would make a pretend pulpit and pews. Gayle was the song leader, and she still is. I was the preacher, and still am. Kathy was the only one who was old enough to read, so that was her job.

Do you remember when preachers used to have someone read for them, and they would repeat it? That's what we would do. Kathy would read it, then with much *self-anointing*, I would repeat it.

Kathy: "God so loved the world"

Me: "GOD SO LOOVVEEDD THE WORLD, THE WHOLE WORLD PEOPLE!"

I get tickled just writing about it! If Gayle wasn't saying amen as many times as I thought she should, I'd yell, "CAN I GET AN AMEN?!" Then she'd wake up and say amen.

Wouldn't it be sad to stand before the Lord and hear Him say, "You were only *playing* church, you were not living it. You were very *dutiful* in your attendance and your giving. But you were never really committed in your service to Me."

Folks, time for playing church is over. Get committed to God. Find a local church that believes in the whole Bible and is full of the Spirit of God. I don't want anyone left behind.

Old Sayings

I grew up hearing my mom and granny James say some things that I didn't fully understand. For instances, if I asked them, "What do you think they are going to do about that?"

Their answer would be, "That's their possum, let 'em wool it." Seriously? Well, I certainly was glad that was all cleared up. NOT!

Now I know you are dying to know how to wool a possum. Remember to tell your friends that this book is educational. This is how they explained it to me.

When a hunter was hunting a possum, many times the possum would climb into a holler (hollow) log. The hunter would get a limb, cut all the leaves off so that it was a slick stick. Then he would run the long limb into the holler log and lay it on the possums back.

Now a possum has long, thin stringy hair. The hunter would begin to wind the stick around and around. The stick would curl the hair around it and the hunter would pull the possum out. Now that my friend, is how you *wool a possum*! I know you've always wanted to do that, right?

During the Great Depression (*not the one we are in now*) in the 1930's, there was a saying going around. Someone would say, "Did you hear about such and such?"

They would reply, "You can hear anything but meat frying in a pan, or money jingling in your pockets!"

We grew up hearing mom say, "Well it's better than a sharp stick in the eye!" I guess so…

I've heard mom say this many times, "They'd complain if they were hung with a new rope!" Maybe…

More than once I heard mom tell us kids, "If you don't stop what you're doing, I'm going to knock both eyes in to one and spit in the hole and call you sap-head!" Okay…

When asked how they were, they would reply, "Fine as a frogs hair split three ways!" Have you ever seen a frogs hair? They are very fine. Now if you split it three ways, you're doing might fine!

I.G.T.S.

When mom would see someone doing something really dumb, she would look at us and say, "That's just I.G.T.S.".

If any one around us ever overheard mom say that, they would not understand what that meant, but we knew. I.G.T.S. means "**Ignorance Gone To Seed!**"

By the way, where is Kingdom come? On several occasions, mom said she was going to send me there!

When Rick, Margie and I were growing up, every adult had what I call, "Whipping rights" on us. Of course Margie never did get any whipping, so I guess I'm really just talking about me and Rick.

"Whipping rights" is when you are in the presence of an adult and you act out, that adult could grab you up and whip you. It didn't matter if it was your aunt or uncle, they didn't even have to be related. It was an unwritten rule. LOL

The Bucket

I remember asking my granny James, "Do you think so and so meant to do that?" She would answer, "I don't know kid. Every ole bucket sits on its own bottom." I felt like breaking out into the song, "I can see clearly now, the rain is gone!" What did that mean, every ole bucket sits on its own bottom?

It means that everyone is accountable for their own actions. When you stand before God you won't be able to blame anyone for what you did, or did not do. You stand on your own feet, or sit on your own bottom!

It amazes me that in today's society how everyone wants to blame everyone else for their own mistakes, or ignorance. I'm still flabbergasted over the woman who drove through McDonalds and spilt her *OWN* hot coffee on her *OWN* self, and sued McDonalds, and won!

People today are afraid to get involved in helping anyone for fear of being sued! You could be a good Samaritan and pull someone from a burning car, just to have *them* sue *you* for pulling their back out of place in the process.

There are video cameras that have caught people in stores spraying water on the floor so they can slip and fall and sue the store. Come on people! Quit trying to get rich quick at someone else's expense. Alright, I'll climb down off my soapbox.

WARSHING CLOTHES

This sounds like something my Granny James would do!

Years ago an Alabama grandmother gave the new bride the following recipe: (This is an exact copy as written and found in an old scrapbook - with spelling errors and all.)

Build fire in backyard to heat kettle of rain water.
Set tubs so smoke wont blow in eyes if wind is pert.
Shave one hole cake of lie soap in boilin' water.
Sort things, make 3 piles
1 pile white,
1 pile colored,
1 pile work britches and rags.
To make starch, stir flour in cool water to smooth, then thin down with boiling water.
Take white things, rub dirty spots on board, scrub hard, and boil, then rub colored. Don't boil just wrench and starch.
Take things out of kettle with broom stick handle, then wrench, and starch.
Hang old rags on fence.
Spread tea towels on grass.
Pore wrench water in flower bed.
Scrub porch with hot soapy water.
Turn tubs upside down.
Go put on clean dress, smooth hair with hair combs...
Brew up a cup of tea, sit and rock a spell and count your blessings.

Paste this over your washer and dryer Next time when you think things are bleak, read it again,
Kiss that washing machine and dryer, and give thanks.
First thing each morning you should run and hug your washer and dryer, also your toilet, those two-holers used to get mighty cold!
For you non-southerners - wrench means, rinse
AND WE THINK WE HAVE IT ROUGH!!!

Life Through the Eyes of a Red Headed, Wide-eyed, Full Time Evangelist!

Hanging with Roy at Patrick Springs, Virginia

Wee, Wee Tot
   Mom used to say, "When I was a wee wee tot, my mom would put me on a wee, wee pot, and tell me to wee wee whether I could or not!

Thanks to Calories
Mom wrote this song to the tune of, "Thanks to Calvary"

Thanks to calories, I'm not the woman I used to be.
Thanks to calories, I'm not skinny any more.
And as the fat rolls on my body, I'm here to tell you,
Thanks to calories, I'm not skinny any more.

Mom's version of Philippians 3:13
   Mom never liked to be considered *fat*, she would rather be thought of as *fluffy*! She struggled with her weight. I can relate. I think that is when she came up with her own definition of this verse:
   "...forgetting those things which are behind, and reaching forth unto those things which are before"
   As she would read, "forgetting those things which are behind," she would point to her weight *behind*.
   Continuing on, "And reaching forth unto those things which are before." That is when she would reach forth and grab a piece of pie!" Like I said, this was her verse, her story and she was sticking to it!
   She also told me that Paul in the Bible was a baker. I said, "I've read the Bible and I've never read anywhere about Paul being a baker. She replied, "He went down to Philippi (fill a pie) didn't he?"

Beat the Child!
   Our mom was a mess, to say the least! She whooped (to whoop is harder than to whip) Rick and I about everyday of our childhood.

She would use the Scripture found in Proverbs 23:13. She would shorten it to, "Beat the child, it shall not die".

Then, she would quote Proverbs 22:15: "Foolishness is bound in the heart of a child; but the rod of correction shall drive it far from him." I often wondered if mom needed to spend more time in the New Testament, you know, where Jesus frequently spoke of *love*!

Frankie, Angie, Adam and Chad

While in church at Harrisburg, my cousin, Frankie, and his wife, Angie, were having a little problem with their son Adam acting out. He was only a year old. Frankie and Angie were sitting on the pew behind mom. Mom leaned back and told Frankie, "I hear it don't hurt to whoop 'em." Frankie still gets a laugh at that when he thinks of it.

That has been twenty something years ago. Frankie and Angie have raised two, well behaved young men, Adam and Chad. Adam is married to a wonderful lady, Erica. And I expect Chad will follow suit. Now the pressure is on, isn't it Chad?

My Last Whooping

I hate to admit this, but I was eighteen-years-old when I got my last whooping. I am not proud of this, but mom thought it necessary, I did not! Margie was thirteen, and it might have been her first whooping. LOL

We were at church in Hoopa, it was a Sunday night. Dad was working away from home, so he was not there (thank the Lord).

Mom was leading song service, I was playing the guitar and Margie was in the congregation. For some odd reason, Margie and I had the giggles, the *uncontrollable* giggles!

If our eyes came into contact with each other, we would both bust out laughing. Fortunately, mom never saw it. This went on throughout the entire song service.

Next, was testimony service. I was still sitting on the platform with my guitar in my hands. All of a sudden I had an urge to look at Margie, to see if she was looking at me. Sort of like that old song, "I was looking back to see, if you were looking back to see, if I was looking back to see, if you were looking back at me."

My mind said, "Don't look!" but I looked anyway. Sure enough, Margie was looking at me, just waiting on me to look at her. Well, we both quietly snickered.

Margie had long blonde hair, and as she went forward to laugh, mom saw what was going on. She grabbed Margie by the hair and jerked her back up to a sitting position. It so shocked Margie, all she could do was say,

"M a m a … !"

Well, that tickled me so much, I had to dismiss myself from the platform! I put my guitar down and walked to the back of the church. I went outside and looked up into the sky and said, "God, You are going to have to help me here. I think mama wants to kill me and Margie. And who knows, I just may grow up to be an Evangelist. I need Your help!"

I went back in, sober-faced. As I went back onto the platform and sat down, I looked at mom. Where was her *smiley face*? It was nowhere to be found.

After church was over, Margie and I ran home (we lived real close to the church). Bonanza was on. About ten minutes later, we heard mom coming up the stairs. They were not *happy* steps either!

She walked in and I said, "Hey mom! You're just in time to watch Bonanza. Isn't Little Joe cute?"

"To the room!" was her response. Margie looked bewildered, but I knew *exactly* what that meant! It meant there was a good chance that we were going to get the tar and nicotine beat out of us!

Once in the bedroom, mom proceeded to remind us that she had *not* raised us to act-up in church!

That went on for what seemed to be an eternity. Then she said, "Now for your punishment!"

Punishment? I thought listening to her go on and on, was our punishment! But she had different thoughts. "You can take a whooping, or you can go to bed right now!" she said.

Well, I was a senior in high school and I wasn't about to go to bed this early! I spoke up and said, "I'll take the whooping!" We looked around to see what Margie was going to say, and she had already jumped in bed!

Mom said, "Get out of bed. Kay already made the decision for you both!"

I was taller than mom and wondered how *she* was going to whoop *me*! She already had it figured out. She told me to lie across the bed. I could see she had put a lot of thought into this.

I laid across the bed and she lit into me with that dadgum board that I thought we had already gotten rid of! I told myself that I wouldn't cry. Boy howdy, it sure was hurting! I finally let out a whimper, and she stopped.

It must have been a full moon that night or I would have never done this. I imitated a popular men's cologne commercial by grabbing her square by the shoulders and saying, "Thanks! I needed that!"

She said, "Oh, you do huh?" and she began whooping me a little bit more. I was trying to dodge her licks, but wasn't being too successful. So I told her I was only kidding.

"Margie, get across that bed!" mom commanded. Margie did. I thought, "You know, this may have all been worth it, just to see Margie get a whooping!" Rick and I always got the whoopings, because, because... we *deserved* them! Mom and dad paid Margie to be good, but Rick and I were good for nothing! Seriously, Margie was a well behaved child growing up. Rick and I were not bad, we were just into things.

Mom raised the board above her head, oh boy, this is what I've been waiting for! She popped Margie good, Margie let out a blood curdling cry. Mom stopped and said, "Now, I hope you two have learned your lesson!"

I couldn't believe it! Margie only got one lick! That was all! I spoke up, "Mom! You gave me a lot of licks, and only gave Margie one! I'll let you whoop me again, if you will just give Margie one like the one you gave me." Mom just shook her head and walked out of the room to watch Bonanza.

All of Margie's childhood, mom could just talk to her and she would begin to cry and apologize. Too bad that didn't work on Rick and me. It was more like a two by four between the eyes, and that was just to get our attention!

Mom was a really great mother. She was our best friend; she played games with us and spent time with us. She loved us *enough* to spank us when we did wrong. Time-out for Rick and me would have been a real joke! Parents today need to love their children as much, and correct them.

Mama use to sing us kids a song. Now that she has gone to Heaven, I sing it to children everywhere I go. I have even had parents call me and say their child wants me to sing it again to them... over the phone! Here is it.

Little Chickie
I had a Little Chickie who wouldn't lay an egg,
So I poured hot water up and down her little leg.
The Little Chickie hollered, and the Little Chickie begged,
Then the Little Chickie laid me a hard-boiled egg!

CHAPTER 14
POPULAR MESSAGES

Turn It Loose!

Old Tom

Tom was a big old yellow cat. He was Billy's best friend and pet. He ate, slept, played, and did everything with Tom. One day Tom was killed, Billy's heart was broken. His world had come to an end.

For two days Billy moped around crying and not eating, while Tom lay on the back porch in the *hot sun*.

Billy's mother finally said, "It's time to bury Tom!" Billy selected a special plot, dug a hole and buried ole Tom. The only problem was, he left Tom's long bushy tail out of the ground.

Every day after school, Billy would run to the grave and *stroke* Tom's old long tail. He would talk to him, reminisce of old times and grieve for his cat.

The family offered Billy any kind of pet to replace Tom, but Billy only wanted Tom.

After a few days, Billy wanted to see Tom *one more time*. He seized his tail, gave him a yank out of the ground, and pulled up the rotted frame of Tom. It was covered with ants and maggots.

Billy yelled when he saw the horrible sight, flung it away, and ran in the house. He was through with Tom! When he saw Tom the way he really was *(dead, corrupt, and rotten)*, he finally gave him up and was finished with him.

We need a move of God that our eyes might be opened. That we too can see some of the things we've been holding on to and even stroking.

Luke 15:20-32

20 And he arose, and came to his father. But when he was yet a great way off, his father saw him, and had compassion, and ran, and fell on his neck, and kissed him.

The reason the father *saw* him is he was *looking* for him! Each morning after prayer, you need to step out on your spiritual porch and look through your spiritual eyes for your loved one who has gone astray. Maybe it's your husband, wife, daughter, son or grandchildren. Don't ever give up on them!

21 And the son said unto him, Father, I have sinned against heaven, and in thy sight, and am no more worthy to be called thy son.
22 But the father said to his servants, Bring forth the best robe, and put it on him; and put a ring on his hand, and shoes on his feet:
23 And bring hither the fatted calf, and kill it; and let us eat, and be merry:
24 For this my son was dead, and is alive again; he was lost, and is found. And they began to be merry.

Take notice when the son confessed, that the father acted as though he never even heard him. Instead, he began making plans for a welcome home party!

When someone *truly repents*, we also should forgive. And maybe even begin to make plans for a party too! Party on!

25 Now his elder son was in the field: and as he came and drew nigh to the house, he heard musick and dancing.
26 And he called one of the servants, and asked what these things meant.

27 And he said unto him, Thy brother is come; and thy father hath killed the fatted calf, because he hath received him safe and sound.
28 And he was angry, and would not go in: therefore came his father out, and entreated him.

Now we deal with the jealous son. I like to call him *Hoss*. As he is coming in from working, he hears a party going on. He asked a servant what was going on. The servant begins to tell Hoss that his brother, *little Joe* had come home. His father was even throwing little Joe a party!

Now, you would think that Hoss would be glad to see little Joe. But the Bible says he was *angry*! Hoss needed to *turn it loose and let it go*. He wouldn't even go into the party!

I can just see Hoss sitting out on the front porch with his arms folded and pouting. Instead of being glad that his brother was finally home, Hoss was angry and refused to go to the party.

Now, I've got to ask you a question. The fact that Hoss did *NOT* go into the party, did it stop the party? No! In fact, everyone continued to *Party On* without him!

THE PARTY DOESN'T STOP JUST BECAUSE YOU REFUSE TO BE A PART OF IT!

One day we are going to the Marriage Supper of the Lamb. If you don't go, we are still going to Party On!

Imagine that your family was planning a family reunion, but you were mad at one of your relatives and refused to go.

At the reunion, someone asks about you, why aren't you there? Someone says, "Well, you know he is mad at his uncle and wouldn't come."

At that moment, does someone at the table stand up and announce, "May I have your attention? The reason Bubba isn't here today, is he is still mad at his uncle.

Now, I want everyone to stop eating, stop having fun and let's all cry."

No, that's not what happens. I can hear that person say, "Wow, that's too bad. Hey, pass some more of that potato salad and fried chicken!"

You may be at home *hoping* that the party will stop. There you are, sulking and feeling sorry for yourself and the party goes on. Party On!

You just need to take your ole *bad self* to the altar and pray though. Then you can go join the party!

> 29 And he answering said to his father, Lo, these many years do I serve thee, neither transgressed I at any time thy commandment: and yet thou never gavest me a kid, that I might make merry with my friends:

Well, well, well! Now he begins to compare himself with his brother. The Bible clearly tells us that by comparing ourselves among ourselves, we are not wise. 2 Cor 10:12

Hoss tells his father how *good* he has been. He tells him how many years he has served him. Then he begins to lie. He tells his father that he has *never* transgressed against him *or* has never broken *any* of his commandments.

Now I tell you, even as good and sweet as I am, (it's alright to laugh) I cannot say that I have *ever* been *that* good! I doubt if any of us have. I say that because I don't want to go down alone!

Hoss then begins to whine about his father never giving him a party with his friends. It's at this point of the story that I wonder if Hoss even had any friends. As for myself, I don't like to hang out with those who complain, whine and are jealous. The older brother was hanging onto several things:

- Bitterness

- Hatred

- Jealousy

- Unforgiveness

INJUSTICE IS ONLY AS *POWERFUL* AS THE *MEMORY* OF IT!

He needed to forget it, turn it loose and *Party On!*

Recently I heard a pastor tell about an electrician who was working in their new church. He was standing on a ladder when he accidentally touched a live wire. He couldn't turn it loose, so he kicked his ladder out from underneath himself. The fall caused him to *turn loose* of the wires.

He had a decision to make as he was being shocked; hang onto the wires and possibly die, or turn it loose and let it go! He turned it loose and let it go, and lived.

Too many people today do not really like hanging onto the *junk* that is killing them, but maybe they are not *desperate* enough to turn it loose and let it go and *live*! It really is as simple as that!

> 30 But as soon as this thy son was come, which hath devoured thy living with harlots, thou hast killed for him the fatted calf.

Did you notice his terminology? He described his brother as *his father's son*. He refused to acknowledge him as his brother. Instead, he said, "But as soon as this *thy son* was come."

So many times when we get mad at someone, we begin to *disrespect* them. I've seen folks get mad at their pastor. Instead of greeting them the way they normally do, they address them with their first name. Instead of, "Hey Pastor!" it's, "Hey Jim."

If it's their boss, they drop the Mr. or Mrs. and just call them by their last name. We need to be careful in disrespecting others. One day that will come back on us.

Hoss continues to berate his brother by reminding his father that little Joe had squandered *his* money with harlots. At this point he becomes even more vicious. He begins to go fishing in the *sea of forgetfulness*.

He begins to drag things *out* that the Heavenly Father has placed *in*, *never* to be *remembered* again! What right do we have to remember what God has forgotten and forgiven? You better turn it loose and let it go so you can Party On!

If someone *truly repents*, even of *this* sin, it is our obligation to forgive them as well, *and* their harlots! Jesus tells us if we don't forgive those who trespass against us, then it ties the hands of God to forgive us our trespasses. I don't know about you, but I need, and want forgiveness!

Let's finish the story...

> 31 And he said unto him, Son, thou art ever with me, and all that I have is thine.
> 32 It was meet that we should make merry, and be glad: for this thy brother was dead, and is alive again; and was lost, and is found.

The father told Hoss that he really never had anything to worry about. His father had enough for both sons. And so it is with our Heavenly Father. "But my God shall supply *all* your need according to his riches in glory by Christ Jesus." Phil 4:19

The father concludes that it was necessary to throw a party because your *brother* was dead, and is alive again; and was lost, and is found. Enough said!

What are you hanging on to?
What are you stroking?
It's time to let it go!
PARTY ON!

"UNITED TOGETHER FOR HIM"
Eph 4:1-3

1 I therefore, the prisoner of the Lord, beseech you that ye walk worthy of the vocation wherewith ye are called,

2 With all lowliness and meekness, with longsuffering, *forbearing one another in love;*

3 Endeavouring to *keep the unity of the Spirit* in the bond of peace.

"STORY ABOUT UNITY"

A rat looked through a crack in the wall to see the farmer and his wife opening a package. What food might it contain? He was aghast to discover that it was a rat trap.

Retreating to the farmyard, the rat proclaimed the warning; "There is a rat trap in the house, there is a rat trap in the house!"

The chicken clucked and scratched, raised her head and said, "Excuse me, Mr. Rat, I can tell this is a grave concern to you, but it is of no consequence to me. I cannot be bothered by it."

The rat turned to the pig and told him, "There is a rat trap in the house, a rat trap in the house!" "I am so very sorry Mr. Rat," sympathized the pig, "but there is nothing I can do about it but pray."

The rat turned to the cow. She said, "Like wow, Mr. Rat, a rat trap. I am in grave danger. Duh?" So the rat returned to the house, head down and dejected, to face the farmer's rat trap alone.

That very night a sound was heard throughout the house, like the sound of a rat trap catching its prey. The farmer's wife rushed to see what was caught.

In the darkness, she did not see that it was an enormous snake whose tail had tripped the trap. The snake bit the farmer's wife.

The farmer rushed her to the hospital. She returned home with a fever. Now everyone knows you treat a fever with fresh chicken soup, so the farmer took his hatchet to the farmyard for the soup's main ingredient, the chicken. He prepared the soup.

His wife's sickness continued so that friends and neighbors came to sit with her around the clock. To feed them the farmer butchered the pig.

The farmer's wife did not get well. She died, and so many people came for her funeral, that the farmer had the cow slaughtered to provide meat for all the many friends to eat.

So the next time you hear that someone is facing a problem and think that it does not concern you, remember that when there is a rat trap in the house, the whole farmyard is at risk!

Phil 2:1-4

1 If there be therefore any consolation in Christ, if any comfort of love, if any fellowship of the Spirit, if any bowels and mercies,

2 Fulfil ye my joy, that ye be likeminded, having the same love, *being of one accord, of one mind.*

3 Let nothing be done through strife or vainglory; but in lowliness of mind let each esteem other better than themselves.

4 Look not every man on his own things, but every man also on the things of others.

Unity ought to be a distinctive mark among Christians. Many people, even Christians, live only to make a good impression on others, or to please themselves. But selfishness brings discord.

Acts 2:1-4

1 And when the day of Pentecost was fully come, they were all with *one accord [UNITY]* in one place.
2 And suddenly there came a sound from heaven as of a rushing mighty wind, and it filled *all* the house where they were sitting.
3 And there appeared unto them cloven tongues like as of fire, and it sat upon each of them.
4 And they were *all* filled with the Holy Ghost, and began to speak with other tongues, as the Spirit gave them utterance.

Acts 2:46-47

46 And they, continuing daily with *one accord* in the temple, and breaking bread from house to house, did eat their meat with gladness and singleness of heart,
47 Praising God, and having favour with *all* the people. And the Lord added to the church daily such as should be saved.

Acts 8:5-8

5 Then Philip went down to the city of Samaria, and preached Christ unto them.
6 And the people with *one accord* gave heed unto those things which Philip spake, hearing and seeing the miracles which he did.
7 For unclean spirits, crying with loud voice, came out of many that were possessed with them: and many taken with palsies, and that were lame, were healed.
8 And there was *great joy* in that city.

I like this story about Unity:

PULL BUDDY, PULL!

An out-of-towner accidentally drove his car into a ditch on a country road. Fortunately, a local farmer came to help with his big strong horse named *Buddy*.

He hitched Buddy up to the car and yelled, "Pull *Nellie*, pull!" Buddy didn't move. Then the farmer hollered, "Pull, *Buster*, pull!" Buddy didn't respond.

Once more the farmer commanded, "Pull, *Coco*, pull!" Nothing. Then the farmer calmly said, *"Pull, Buddy, pull!"* And the horse easily dragged the car out of the ditch.

The motorist was most appreciative and very curious. He asked the farmer why he had called his horse by the wrong name three times.

"Well, Buddy is *blind* and if he thought he was the only one pulling, *he wouldn't even try!*"

We need *Spiritual blinders* on and quit worrying about what everyone else is doing, and simply do what GOD wants *YOU* to do!

My Mom used to plow with mules that had blinders on them. blinders are to keep them from being distracted.

Don't get distracted. Do what God wants *you* to do and that's it. We concern ourselves too much with what everyone else is doing.

John 17:20-23

20 Neither pray I for these alone, but for them also which shall believe on me through their word;

21 That they all may be *one*; as thou, Father, *art in me, and I in thee,* that they also may be *one* in us: that the world may believe that thou hast sent me.

22 And the glory which thou gavest me I have given them; that they may be *one*, even as we are *one*:

23 I in them, and thou in me, that they may be made perfect in *one*; and that the world may know that thou hast sent me, and hast loved them, as thou hast loved me.

Instead of being a church on *LIFE SUPPORT*, we need to be a *SPIRITUAL EMERGENCY ROOM*.

A place of rescue for those who feel crushed by the darkness of this world.

Lord, please help us to become united with You and one another!

CHAPTER 15
MY FAVORITE RECIPES

KAY'S BAR-B-Q SAUCE OVER OVEN BAKED CHICKEN
Salt and pepper boneless chicken (or what-ever meat)
Roll it in flour
Melt ½ stick butter in baking pan
Roll chicken in it, place in oven at 350 for 30 minutes

In an iron skillet, mix the following and cook over low
Heat for 30 minutes while stirring.
1 bottle of honey barbeque sauce
1 cup brown sugar
½ cup grape jelly
1 tbsp of vinegar
Squirt of mustard
1/3 cup of honey
½ finely chopped onion

After chicken has cooked for 30 minutes,
Turn it over and pour sauce over it and cook for an additional 30 minutes.

******

Kay's Deer Steak & Gravy (Quinton's favorite)
Homemade gravy:
In a sauce pan put 2 cups of milk, sprinkle Lowry's season salt and pepper in it and heat on low.
Melt a half stick of butter in a cup (microwave), stir in flour until it is the consistency of toothpaste.
Stir this in the heated milk until smooth and hot. Sit aside.

Salt and pepper deer, roll in flour and fry. Take it up and pour grease out. Place 2 cans of cream of mushroom soup in skillet along with homemade gravy. Stir together under medium heat, then add deer and simmer 15 minutes.

Jessie's Banana Nut Frosting and Cake

My mother, Jessie Osban, created this frosting to put on the Banana Nut Donuts that the local church in Hoopa use to make. It is wonderful and it is fatting! Eater, beware!

Bake a french vanilla cake mix, let it cool while you make the frosting.

FROSTING:

Pinch 3 small bananas (or 2 large) in bite size portions into a mixing bowl.
Add 1-½ sticks of butter (or margarine) that is room temperature, *do not melt*.
Add one box of powered sugar and 1 tablespoon of vanilla.
Mix together well with a blender.
Sometimes I put it on the cake while the cake is warm.
But the best way is to let the frosting *set up* in the refrigerator for an hour.
After you frost the cake, add lots of chopped (not finely chopped) *walnuts*.

"BOB'S BLACK BEANS AND RICE"
(Brother Davis created this and it is so good!)

Bell Peppers, one each: red, green and yellow
3 Carrots
3 Celery Sticks
3 Beef Bouillon Cubes
1 Large Onion
3 or 4 12 oz. Glasses of Water
½ Bottle (small) of Tabasco Sauce (or less)
2 Hickory Smoked all Beef Sausage
3 cans of Ranch Style Black Beans (Wal-Mart)

Cook down until vegetables are tender (about 1 hour). Serve over white rice.

FUDGE PECAN PIE
I use to make this for daddy, and he loved it!

1/4 cup cocoa

3 eggs

1 cup sugar

½ cup corn syrup

1/4 cup melted butter

1 cup pecans

Beat eggs slightly in a 2 quart bowl.

Stir in sugar, syrup, cocoa, butter and pecans.

Pour into un-baked pie shell

(Cover edges of shell with foil)

Bake near center of oven @ 375 for 1 hour. Yum!

******

KEY LIME CAKE BY MARLENE HULETT (CAUTION: THIS CAKE IS ADDICTIVE!)

1 box Duncan Hines lemon supreme cake mix
1- 3 oz box lime Jell-O
1 cup Wesson oil
3/4 cup orange juice
5 eggs
Sift all above ingredients and bake 20-25 minutes at 350. It makes 3 to 4 layers.

After layers are cooled from hot to warm, drizzle them with 1/3 cup key lime juice and ½ cup confectioners' sugar (mixed together)

Frosting:
16 oz. Cream cheese (softened)
2 sticks butter (softened)
2 boxes confectioners' sugar
2 tsp vanilla
2 cups pecans
You will have frosting left over. Refrigerate cake after a day.

******

RHUBARB PIE
Ingredients:
4 cups chopped rhubarb
1-1/3 cups white sugar
6 Tbs. all purpose flour
1 Tbs. butter
9" pie crust
Sprinkle Rhubarb with salt
Baking directions:
Preheat oven to 450 degrees.
Combine sugar and flour.
Sprinkle 1/4 of sugar and flour over pastry in pie plate.
You can also add a spoon of instant Tapioca if desired.
Heap the rhubarb over the sugar and flour in the pie plate.
Add remaining sugar and flour over the rhubarb.
Dot with butter.
Cover rhubarb pie with other pie crust.
Bake 15 minutes at 450 degrees and then reduce heat to 350 degrees and cook for one hour longer, until pie crust is brown.

This Author also has a singing CD titled,
"21 Southern Gospel Songs as Sung by Kay Osban"
They are $10 each.
She can be contacted at:
912-467-8188
Osban55@yahoo.com

This picture is nostalgic to me. When I first began, I made an LP vinyl record, then the good ole eight-track, then the cassettes. I finally progressed to the CD!

Another Good Book to Read:

"Your Dreams Will Come to Pass"
By Andrea Richardson Taylor.

She can be contacted at:
AndreaRichardsonTaylor@gmail.com

Made in the USA
Charleston, SC
18 March 2016